QUEST

A World of Change
1900–2000
Activity Support Guide

Alan Coulson • Jess Harris

Stanley Thornes (Publishers) Ltd

First published in 2000 by:
Stanley Thornes (Publishers) Ltd
Delta Place
27 Bath Road
CHELTENHAM GL53 7TH
United Kingdom

00 01 02 03 04 / 10 9 8 7 6 5 4 3 2 1

A catalogue record for this book is available from the British Library.

ISBN 0-7487-4285-9

Acknowledgements

The authors and publishers are grateful to the following for permission to use photographs and other copyright material in this book:

Camera Press 147 (right), 148 (top & bottom); Coventry Evening Telegraph 129; Hulton Getty 15, 16 (right), 55, 132, 134 (top), 147 (left), 148 (middle), 171; Imperial War Museum 134 (bottom), 135; National Monuments Record 16 (left); Newcastle Evening Chronicle 122; Popperfoto 84.

© The Guardian for the adapted article by J Sweeney featured in the Observer, p.47; Copyright Siegfried Sassoon by kind permission of George Sassoon, p.50.

Every effort has been made to contact copyright holders. The publishers apologise to anyone whose rights have been inadvertently overlooked, and will be happy to rectify any errors or omissions.

Page layout by Janet McCallum
Edited by Melanie Gray
Illustrated by Hardlines and Angela Lumley
Cover artwork by Beverly Curl

Printed and bound in Great Britain by Ashford Colour Press, Gosport, Hampshire

Contents

Contents *continued*

Aims
- To stimulate pupils' interest in history;
- To help pupils increase their knowledge and understanding of the 20th-century world;
- To help pupils deepen their understanding of historical skills (Knowledge, skills and understanding).

The activities
This Activity Support Guide contains a wide variety of worksheets prepared with OfSTED in mind and based on the principle of active learning.

The activities range from basic comprehension to imaginative role-play situations. Some are diagram-based, using shapes, sizes and arrows as tools to convey an understanding of significance, extent, direction and linkage in the past. Most worksheets reflect the growing trend of a return to a narrative story-telling approach to the teaching of history, and thus the amount of source-based work is kept to a minimum. All worksheets are based on National Curriculum Knowledge, skills and understanding.

Differentiation
Throughout each chapter, the worksheets have been designed to reflect three broad ability ranges and are labelled accordingly:

A For pupils of below average ability;
B For pupils of average ability;
C For pupils of above average ability.

The matching of worksheets to differing ability ranges has been designed mainly on the basis of 'differentiation by input' and considers:

- the degree of difficulty of the topic;
- the amount of information involved;
- the style and scope of questions;
- the language level required;
- the location of information involved.

All worksheets reflect appropriate National Curriculum levels.

How to use the worksheets
The worksheets have clear, step-by-step instructions to guide pupils. They have been designed mainly for whole-class teaching and there are opportunities for group/pair work. Most activities are suitable for double lessons, whilst a minority fit into a single period. The pupils' book is needed for many worksheets, but some are free-standing and are useful for homework.

Formative assessment guidance sheet

Below are some suggestions on which to assess pupil responses to the worksheets in this Activity Support Guide. The table has been designed to make assessment straightforward for teachers and easy for pupils to understand.

Standard	Quality	Quantity	Grade/mark		
Excellent/ Very good	All or nearly all appropriate items included	Very detailed	A	9–10	17–20
Good	Most appropriate items included	Detailed	B	7–8	13–16
Satisfactory	About half appropriate items included	Some details	C	5–6	9–12
Poor	Some appropriate items included	Outline	D	3–4	5–8
Very poor	A few appropriate items included	Broad outline	E	1–2	1–4
				10	20

Worksheet		Knowledge, skills and understanding				
		1	2	3	4	5
Introduction to *Quest 4*	A		✓		✓	
	B		✓		✓	
	C		✓		✓	
1 A new era	A	✓	✓		✓	
	ABC	✓	✓		✓	✓
	BC	✓	✓		✓	✓
3 The Suffragettes	A		✓			✓
	B		✓		✓	
	C		✓		✓	
4 Background to the First World War	A		✓			
	A	✓	✓			
	B		✓			✓
	C		✓		✓	
5 The two sides	A			✓		
7 The Home Front	B		✓		✓	
	C		✓	✓	✓	
8 War at sea and in the air	A		✓			
	B		✓			
	C		✓	✓	✓	
9 Trench warfare and the Western Front	A	✓	✓			
	A		✓			✓
	B		✓	✓	✓	
	B		✓			✓
	C		✓	✓	✓	
	C		✓		✓	✓
10 The end of the First World War	A		✓			
	B		✓	✓		✓
	C		✓		✓	✓
	B		✓			✓
	C		✓			
	ABC		✓		✓	✓
11 Peace-making and peace-keeping	A		✓			✓
	A		✓			✓
	B		✓			✓
	B		✓			✓
	C		✓			
	C		✓			✓
12 The USA, 1918–1939	A		✓		✓	✓
	B		✓		✓	✓
	C		✓		✓	✓
	ABC	✓	✓			✓
	ABC	✓	✓			✓
	ABC					✓
13 Boom then crash	A		✓			✓
	AB		✓		✓	
	ABC		✓		✓	
	AB		✓		✓	
	AB		✓		✓	✓
	C		✓		✓	
	C		✓		✓	✓
14 President Roosevelt and the New Deal	A		✓			
	AB		✓			
	C		✓		✓	
15 Tsarist rule in Russia	A		✓		✓	
	B		✓		✓	
	C	✓	✓	✓	✓	

Worksheet		Knowledge, skills and understanding				
		1	2	3	4	5
16 The Russian Revolution	A		✓			✓
17 Lenin in power	A	✓	✓		✓	
	B		✓	✓	✓	
	B	✓	✓		✓	✓
	C		✓		✓	✓
	C	✓	✓		✓	✓
18 Stalin in power	ABC	✓	✓		✓	✓
20 Germany	A		✓			
	A		✓			✓
	B		✓			✓
	B		✓		✓	
	C		✓			
	C		✓		✓	✓
21 The road to war	A		✓			✓
	B		✓			✓
	C		✓		✓	✓
22 War in Europe	A		✓		✓	✓
	A		✓			
	B		✓			
	C		✓			✓
23 War in Britain	A		✓		✓	
	A		✓			
	B		✓			✓
	B		✓			✓
	C		✓			
	C		✓			✓
24 The widening war	A		✓			
	B		✓		✓	✓
	C		✓		✓	✓
25 Major turning points	A		✓		✓	✓
	B		✓		✓	✓
	C		✓	✓	✓	✓
26 The secret war	A		✓			✓
	B		✓			✓
	C		✓		✓	✓
	ABC		✓			
27 Blockade and bombs	A		✓			✓
	B		✓		✓	✓
	C		✓	✓		✓
28 The end of the Third Reich	A		✓			
	B		✓			
	C		✓		✓	✓
29 The end of the Second World War	A		✓			✓
	B		✓			✓
	C		✓		✓	✓
	A		✓			✓
	ABC		✓		✓	✓
30 Towards Cold War	A		✓			
	B		✓			✓
	C		✓	✓		✓
31 The Cold War	A		✓			
	B		✓			✓
	C		✓			✓
Conclusion to *Quest 4*	A		✓		✓	
	B				✓	
	C		✓		✓	

You will need

A Introduction to the textbook

1 Look at the contents pages at the front of the textbook.

    a How many chapters are there altogether?

    b How many pages are there altogether?

    c Using the chapter titles only, how many chapters deal with fighting between countries?

    d Using the chapter titles only, how many chapters deal with peace between countries?

    e Find five other topics from the chapter titles and write them in the table below.

Topic	Chapter number

2 Look at the index at the back of the textbook.
    a Find the names of any ten people listed and write them in the table below.

Name of person	Male/female

    b Using the information from your table, who do you think were more important in the 20th century, men or women?

B A look at the textbook

1 Look at the contents pages. Use the information there to complete the table below.

Topic	Number of chapters
International events	
Britain	
USA	
USSR	
Germany	

2 Using the information in the table, which topics do you think will be the most important?

_____

3 Using the information in the table, which topics do you think will be the least important?

_____

4 Look at the index and, choosing four people you are interested in, use the information there to complete the table below.

Name of person	Number of pages	Name of person	Number of pages

5 Which person/people seems to be the most important?

_____

6 Look at the front cover of the book and describe the topics on the screens.

_____

_____

7 Look again at the contents pages. Which topics/chapters does the front cover best match up with?

_____

C What are we going to study?

1 Look at the contents pages and complete the table below.

Contents	Number of chapters	Total number of pages
First World War		
Second World War		
Cold War		
Britain		
USA		
USSR		
Germany		
Ordinary people's lives		

2 Using the information in the table, which topics do you think will be the most important in the 20th century?

_____

_____

3 Using the information in the table, which topics do you think will be the least important in the 20th century?

_____

4 Write a sentence to explain how you chose your topics for Questions 2 and 3.

_____

_____

5 Do you think the contents are organised in topics, chronologically, or both? Explain how you reached your decision.

_____

_____

6 Look at the front cover of the book. Why do you think the author chose this particular illustration?

 C **What are we going to study? (continued)**

7 Look at the index and choose eight people you are interested in.

Name of person	Politician/ soldier/ inventor	Number of pages	Tick the six most important people

8 Look at several double pages in the book. What separate items does each double page have (e.g. illustrations)?

_____

_____

9 Look again at your answer to Question 8. Why do you think the pages have these items?

_____

_____

10 Find some historical terms used in the book (for example, dictatorship, communism). Write down a few below and explain their meanings.

Terms	Explanations

A *Healthy eating?*

Look at page 5 in your textbook.

1   Edward VII started his day with a huge breakfast.

Porridge and cream   Scones   Eggs, bacon, sausages and kidney

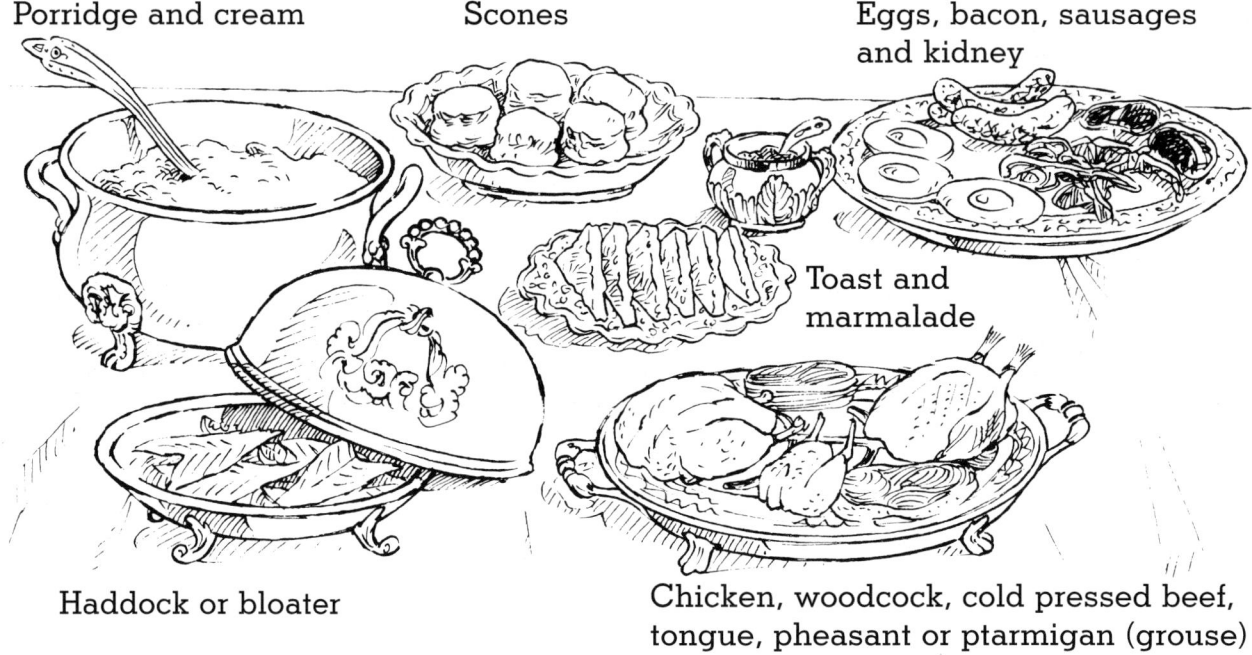

Toast and marmalade

Haddock or bloater

Chicken, woodcock, cold pressed beef, tongue, pheasant or ptarmigan (grouse)

Although many people would have liked to have enjoyed a breakfast as grand as Edward's, only those with a great deal of money could do so.

Make up your own breakfast table with the sorts of things we might eat today.

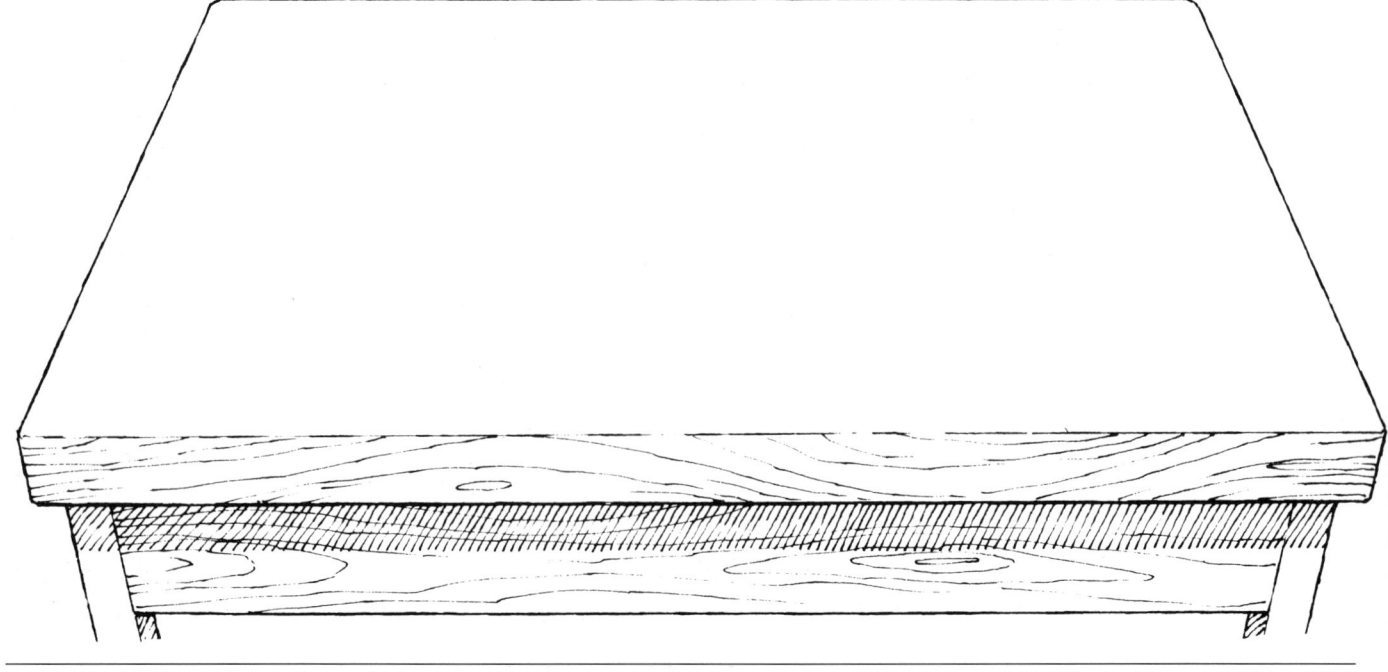

A Healthy eating? (continued)

2 Most people in Britain in 1900 did not have the same income as Edward VII.

Rich

Poor

Upper class: 2 per cent of the population, income about £1,000 a year. Earls, dukes, army and navy officers.

Middle class: 25 per cent of the population, income between £150 and £1,000 a year. Judges, doctors, lawyers and professionals.

Working class: 73 per cent of the population, income £100 a year or less. Poor servants, miners, factory workers, labourers, blacksmiths, railway workers, shopworkers, street sellers, etc.

Does income or what a person does for a living decide what class they belong to today?

3 In 1901 Seebohm Rowntree looked at the lives of poor people in York. In his report he said that many poor people lived below the 'poverty line' (the minimum amount that a person would need to be able to live). He said that:

- a single man would need at least 7 shillings (35p) a week.
- a married man with a wife and three children would need at least 21 shillings and 8 pence (£1.09) a week.

Weekly spending on food by a working man, his wife and five children in York, 1901 (not including heating, lighting, rent, insurance, clothing, cleaning stuffs)

20lb flour (for bread)	1s 10d
4lb wheatmeal (for bread and porridge)	4d
Yeast	2d
1lb butter	10d
3lb bacon	1s 0d
6oz tea	6d
1lb currants	3d
1lb lard	4d
2lb fish	6d
Onions	1d
4lb beef	1s 7d
7lb potatoes	2d
8 eggs	6d
Cabbage	2d
Total	**8s 3d (41p)**

 Healthy eating? (continued)

a Study the shopping list on the previous page. Is there anything on it that we tend not to buy today?

_____

b Add some foods that you buy regularly which are not on this list.

_____

c Look at the things you have added to the shopping list. Do you think these were not on the original list because they were not available in 1901 or because people could not afford them?

_____

d Using the original shopping list, draw a meal for a poor person on the table below.

e Look again at Question 1. Which foods from Edward's breakfast table would poor people be able to afford? Make a list below.

_____

4 We have a lot more choice than Edwardians in the food we can buy today. Think of some reasons why and write them down below.

_____

14

ABC Healthy living?

Look at page 7 in your textbook.

Study Sources **A** and **B** below, which show two families at the turn of the 20th century.

1   Next to each source, describe what you can see. Use the words in the Word box to help you.

2   Decide which picture shows a poor family and which shows a rich family and write 'Rich family' or 'Poor family' in the boxes above.

Source A
▼

Word box
clothes • furniture • children
• adults • clean • tidy • dirty • sick
• well • happy • thin • untidy • old
• worn • neat • mouldy • smoky

This family is

_____

_____

_____

_____

_____

_____

Source B
▼

This family is

_____

_____

_____

_____

_____

_____

_____

 *Rich and poor in the 1900s*

Look at page 5 in your textbook.

1   Study the sources below and answer the questions on the next sheet.

Source A An Edwardian upper-class household

▼

Source B A working-class family in the early years of the 20th century

▼

Source C From *Poverty: A Study of Town Life* by Seebohm Rowntree, 1901

▼

[They] must never spend a penny on railway fare or omnibus. They must never go into the country unless they walk. They must never purchase a halfpenny newspaper or spend a penny to buy a ticket for a popular concert... The children must have no pocket money for dolls, marbles or sweets. The father must smoke no tobacco, and must drink no beer. The mother must never buy any pretty clothes for herself or for her children... Finally, the wage earner must never be absent from his work for a single day. If any of these conditions are broken, the extra expenditure involved is met, and can only be met, by limiting the diet.

Source D By Arthur Ponsonby in *The Camel and the Needle's Eye*, 1909

▼

In a house consisting of a living-room, bedroom and a small scullery live father, mother, three sons, also three children under ten and two men lodgers. Seven sleep in the bedroom... and five sleep in the living-room... The landlord and the lord of the manor of this district lives with his wives and family in a house containing over one hundred rooms, and is attended by a staff of 44 indoor servants. He has the choice of three other country residences and a town house, and owns over 186,000 acres.

Source E Adapted from the Royal Commission report, *Poor Laws and Relief of Distress, 1905–1909*

▼

Our investigations prove the existence amongst us of a class whose health and living conditions are a danger to the whole country... No country, however, rich, can permanently hold its own in the race of international competition if hampered by an increasing load of this dead weight; or can successfully run an overseas empire if its own folk at home are sinking below the civilisation of its subject races abroad.

BC Rich and poor in the 1900s (continued)

2 Using Source **A**, list the things that you can see which make you think that the family led comfortable lives.

_____

_____

3 Did the people in Source **A** have servants? How do you know?

_____

_____

4 What are the differences between Sources **A** and **B**?

_____

_____

5 What do you conclude about the incomes of the two families and their place in society?

_____

_____

6 Study Source **D**. What comparison does Ponsonby make between the living conditions of rich and poor people?

_____

_____

7 In 1902 the army turned down two out of every three recruits because they were unfit. Britain had a huge empire at that time. Why should the government be worried about the Royal Commission report (Source **E**)?

_____

_____

8 Using the evidence you have gathered, write your own report on the class differences in Edwardian society.

_____

_____

_____

A Votes for women

Look at page 17 in your textbook, which will give you some ideas about why people thought that women should have been able to vote in elections and help to choose governments.

Read the information below, which will give you some ideas about why people thought that women should not have been able to vote.

> A woman's place has always been at home, looking after the house and the family.

> A man's place had always been at work, earning money for the family.

> Not all men are allowed to vote, so why should any woman be allowed to?

> Anyone who can vote should be able to become an MP. Government is too tough for women.

Decide whether you think women **should** or **should not** have been allowed to vote in 1900. Design a poster either for votes for women or against votes for women. Use a sheet of plain A4 paper for your poster. Below are some ideas to help you with your design.

1 Include a drawing (for example, of women holding banners) or use symbols such as a ballot (voting) box.
2 Include a slogan – a title in words which explains what your poster is about.
3 Use colour to make your poster look more attractive.

You will need

B Suffragettes

Look at pages 17, 19 and 20 in your textbook.

1 From page 17, list as many reasons as you can find why women began to campaign to get the vote.

_____

_____

_____

_____

_____

_____

2 In 1903 Emmeline Pankhurst and her daughter formed the Women's Social and Political Union (WSPU) to campaign for votes for women. Why might getting the vote make women's lives better?

_____

_____

_____

_____

_____

3 From pages 19 and 20, complete the boxes below and on the next sheet.

Suffragettes and the law

_____

_____

_____

_____

_____

_____

_____

_____

You will need

B Suffragettes (continued)

Actions taken by Suffragettes in the first few years

_____
_____
_____
_____
_____

Actions taken by Suffragettes in the later years

_____
_____
_____
_____
_____

4   You will have noticed that the boxes are not in chronological order. Write the number 1 at the top of the box containing the events that happened first, 2 at the top of the box containing events that happened next, and 3 at the top of the box containing events that happened last.

5   What do you think was the Suffragettes' most daring action?

_____
_____

6   Had the Suffragettes gained the vote for women by 1914?

_____

7   Write down any reasons you can think of to explain your answer to Question 6.

_____
_____
_____

You will need

Suffragists and Suffragettes

Look at pages 18, 19 and 32 in your textbook.

1   Read the information below.

> Women had few rights in the 19th century. They were not able to own property, there were hardly any girls, schools and career opportunities were limited. Some women saw gaining the vote and influencing governments as the only way to a better life.

2   Complete the following table.

	Suffragists	Suffragettes
Organisations formed		
Actions taken		

You will need

C | Suffragists and Suffragettes (continued)

3 Compare the actions taken by the Suffragists and the Suffragettes. Which group do you think did the most to try to help women in gaining the vote? Explain your answer.

_____

_____

_____

_____

_____

_____

4 List some of the jobs women did for the first time during the First World War.

_____

_____

_____

_____

_____

_____

_____

_____

5 Shade those jobs that needed skill in one colour, and those that required physical strength in another colour.

6 In 1918 women over 30 were given the vote. What won the vote for women: protest or co-operation? Explain your answer.

_____

_____

_____

_____

_____

You will need

A The enemies and the arguments

Look at pages 6 and 21 in your textbook.

1 a Use the information on page 6 to complete the table below.

Name of countries	Date	Name of alliance

b Choose two colours. Shade the British side's alliances in one colour, and the German side's alliances in another colour.

2 Use the information on page 21 to fill in the missing words in the paragraph below. Use the words in the box at the bottom.

The German side was called the Triple _____ and the British side was called the Triple _____. In 1906 an arms race began between Britain and Germany when Britain launched a super-battleship called the _____. The ruler of Germany was the _____. He wanted his country to have an _____ overseas, just like Britain and France. In 1905 and 1911 he tried to cause trouble with _____ over her African colony, _____. These events helped to make Britain and France enemies of Germany.

> **Word box**
> empire • Entente • Dreadnought • Morocco • Kaiser • France • Alliance

You will need

 A *Murder at Sarajevo*

Look at page 22 in your textbook.

1 Number each information box below in chronological order (write the number 1 at the top of the box dealing with the earliest event, 2 at the top of the next box, and so on).

2 Cut out the boxes and stick them onto a plain sheet of paper in chronological order (1 to 8).

The third terrorist, Nedjelko Cabrinovic, is on Cumurja Bridge along Appel Quay. He throws a bomb which lands under the third car, injuring the passengers and driver.	The driver takes a wrong turning up Franz Joseph Street and has to reverse back. At this moment the fourth terrorist, Gavrilo Princip, who is standing nearby, shoots and kills the Duke and his wife.
Princip is arrested by police. He is later beaten up in jail.	Franz Ferdinand and his wife, Sophia, arrive at Sarajevo railway station at 9.30am.
The Duke and his wife get into a dark-green, open-topped car. It is the second car in a line of six outside the station.	At the town hall it is decided that Sophia and the Duke will return to the station by a different route. The driver is not told.
The remaining five cars drive quickly to the town hall. They are too quick for the other three terrorists to do anything.	The first two terrorists are on Appel Quay near the station. When the cars drive past they take fright and do nothing.

You will need
Dictionary

B How did the First World War start?

Look at pages 21 to 23 in your textbook.

1   Write the names of the two alliances and the six countries involved in these alliances in the boxes below.

| 1882
The Triple _____ | 1907
The Triple _____ |

Name of nation _____

- Had world's best army.
- Wanted to keep recent land gains in Europe.
- Wanted an empire overseas – needed to expand navy.

Name of nation _____

- Wanted to recover land lost recently in Europe.
- Wanted greater power and wealth by gaining an empire overseas.
- Needed allies.

Name of nation _____

- Was a country of many different races.
- Wanted to keep her Balkan Empire of Slav peoples.

Name of nation _____

- Was a huge, but backward, country.
- Needed to modernise industry and increase trade with Europe.
- As a Slav country, wanted to protect Balkan Slavs.

Name of nation _____

- Was a recently formed country.
- Was poor and wanted to create wealth and power by gaining an overseas empire.

Name of nation _____

- Had world's best navy.
- Was world's richest country.
- Wanted to maintain empire overseas.

2   Draw lines from any four dots on the left-hand side to any four dots on the right-hand side where you think clashes between the two sides could have happened.

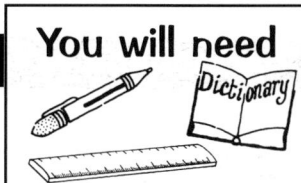

You will need

B *How did the First World War start?*
(continued)

3   Look at the four lines you have drawn for Question 2. Use
     these and the information in your textbook to write two
     sentences about each of the clashes.

     Clash 1 _____

     _____

     Clash 2 _____

     _____

     Clash 3 _____

     _____

     Clash 4 _____

     _____

4   Use the information on page 23 in your textbook to complete
     the table below.

Nation declaring war	Nation war declared on
on	
on	
on	
on	

5   Look up the terms 'ultimatum' and 'mobilisation' in a
     dictionary. Write a sentence to explain each term below.

     Ultimatum _____

     _____

     Mobilisation _____

     _____

C *Why did the First World War break out?*

Look at pages 21 to 23 in your textbook.

1   Complete the diagram below.

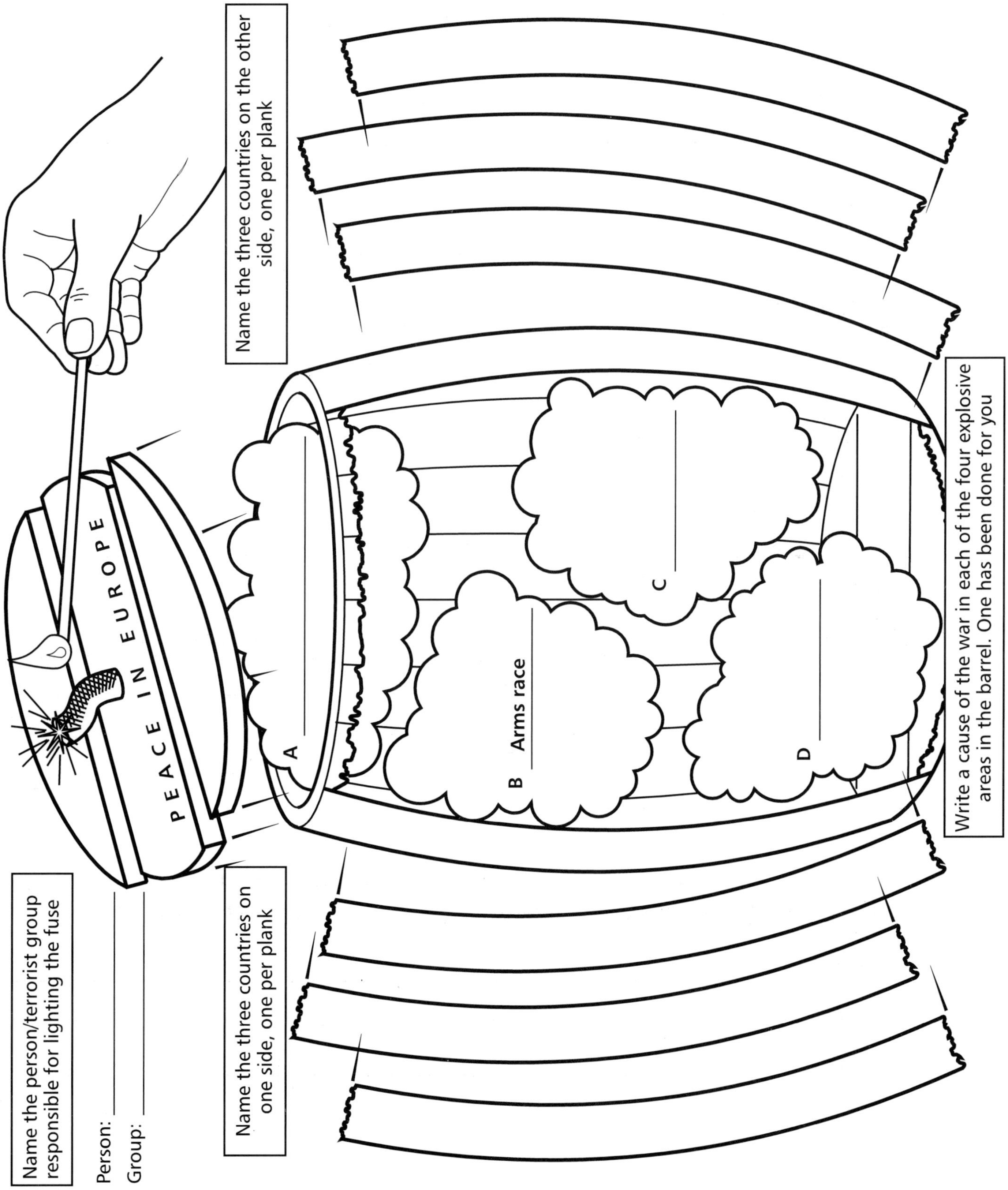

Name the three countries on the other side, one per plank

PEACE IN EUROPE

Write a cause of the war in each of the four explosive areas in the barrel. One has been done for you

A

B   Arms race

C

D

Name the person/terrorist group responsible for lighting the fuse

Person: _____

Group: _____

Name the three countries on one side, one per plank

C Why did the First World War break out? (continued)

2   Look again at the four causes of war you have placed in the barrel. Using information from your textbook, complete the writing frames below.

Cause A

Details

Why this helped cause the war

| |
| |
| |
| |
| |
| |

Cause B

Details   Arms race

Why this helped cause the war   Countries with a lot of weapons believe

they can win a war and are therefore more liable to fight.

| |
| |
| |
| |
| |

Cause C

Details

Why this helped cause the war

| |
| |
| |
| |
| |
| |

C | *Why did the First World War break out? (continued)*

Cause D
Details
Why this helped cause the war

3   Write down the names of the two sides at the start of the war.

_____

_____

4   Both sides should share the blame for causing the First World War. Write down what you think each major power could be blamed for.

Major power	Blamed for

5   Which side do you think was *mainly* to blame? Explain your answer.

_____

_____

_____

_____

_____

You will need

A Should we join up?

Look at pages 24 and 25 in your textbook.

1 Read the information below.

> In August 1914 Britain did not have enough soldiers to defeat Germany, so the government tried to persuade men to volunteer to join up. This is known as a recruitment campaign. Men who did enlist and wore their uniforms were often cheered by others. Those who did not enlist were sometimes given a white feather to show that they were thought of as cowards.

2 a Cut out the boxes, machine-guns and feathers below.

   b Stick the boxes that show that men **would fight** onto a plain piece of paper under the heading 'Would fight'. Stick a machine-gun next to each box.

   c Stick the boxes that show men **would not fight** onto the same piece of paper under the heading 'Would not fight'. Stick a white feather next to each box.

The war will give me a chance to see the world and kill the enemy.	All my friends have joined up. I do not want to be left out.	According to my religion, it is wrong to kill people.
I think it is an honour to serve my King and my country.	I have always believed that arguments should be sorted out by talking.	I have a well-paid job. It would be a pity to leave it.
I have a large family and my wife is not very well.	If I do not join up people will think I'm scared.	I think the world would be a better place if the Germans are beaten.

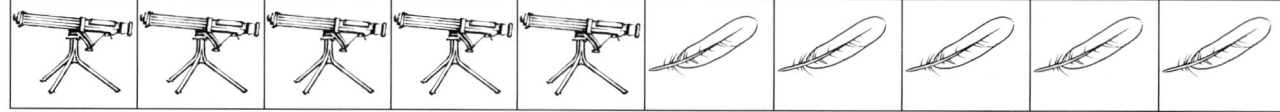

3 Look at the recruitment figures on page 25 in your textbook.

   a Did the recruitment campaign work? _____

   b Write a sentence to explain your answer to Question 3a.

_____

_____

You will need

B Problems and solutions

Look at pages 30 and 32 in your textbook.

1   Read the information below.

> The purposes of German air raids were to hit military targets (to reduce production) and to hit civilians (to weaken the will to fight). It was not until September 1916 that the first Zeppelin was shot down. The first air raids by aeroplanes took place in 1917. Aeroplanes caused more deaths and damage than airships throughout the raids on England.
>
> In 1914 most of Britain's food supply came from abroad. German U-boats sank many ships carrying supplies to Britain. Many shops ran out of food and some people began to hoard. Food prices rose sharply. A government campaign to get people to conserve food was followed in 1917 by rationing. Also, prices of home-grown food such as potatoes were fixed by the government. In 1914 nearly 1.2 million men volunteered to fight, leaving their peace-time jobs. After that, about 100,000 men joined up each month. Eventually, in 1916, men were forced to fight when conscription was introduced.

2   Using the textbook and the information above, complete the diagram below.

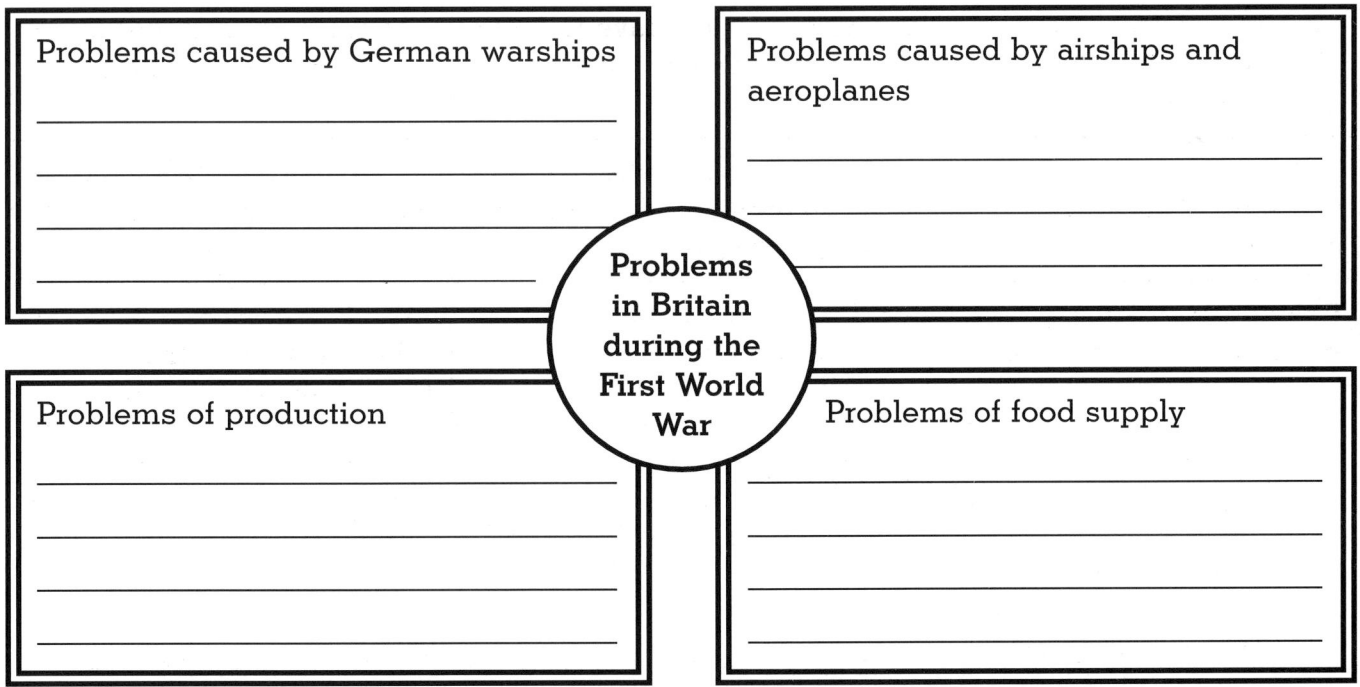

3   Choose two colours. Shade around the edges of the boxes that have details of civilian deaths in one colour. Shade around the edges of the boxes concerned with industry and agriculture in the other colour.

B Problems and solutions (continued)

4 Using the textbook and the information on the previous sheet, complete the diagram below.

Solutions to German warships	Solutions to airships and aeroplanes

Solutions to the problems in Britain during the First World War

Solutions to production	Solutions to food supply

5 Look again at the solution boxes above, and then at these labels:

political • economic • social • religious • military

Decide which label best describes the contents in each box and write the details below.

Solutions to German warships   _____

Solutions to airships and airoplanes   _____

Solutions to production   _____

Solutions to food supply   _____

 Censorship and propaganda

Look at pages 30 and 31 in your textbook.

1 Read the censorship rules below.

Censorship rules
1 Do not mention numbers of British troops or where they are prior to a battle.
2 Do not mention British battle plans.
3 Avoid any mention of British casualties/defeats.

---

2 a Imagine you are a censor during the First World War. Using the censorship rules, cross out any information in the extract below that you think should not appear in a British newspaper report. The extract is about the first day of the Battle of the Somme in 1916.

Morning
The mine in front of Beaumont Hamel was blown up, which gave waiting German troops the knowledge of an imminent attack.
At zero hour, the week-long barrage on German trenches, involving 1.5 million shells, ended. The British forces went 'over the top', walking at a steady pace (as instructed) across no man's land.
The artillery barrage had not worked and German machine-guns opened upon British troops. The barbed wire was virtually intact on German trenches.
Further waves of infantry followed, and those few who reached German trenches showed great courage and skill in hand-to-hand fighting.
Three divisions attained almost all their objectives and were fighting towards Montauban. One of the divisions reached the reserve trenches near Thiepval. However, the troops at Beaumont Hamel suffered 91 per cent casualties.
Afternoon
Mametz fell to one division after a hard fight. The division, which had taken its objective at Gommecourt, was forced back to the trenches it had left.
Results
The first day of the Somme resulted in the highest ever casualties for the British army: 60,000 wounded or killed. There were some gains of about 3km in the sector between the River Somme and Albert.

---

b Look again at your censorship. Approximately what proportion of the details have you crossed out?

 C *Censorship and propaganda (continued)*

> **Propaganda**
> Aim: To stir up anti-German feelings among the British public.
> Methods: To exaggerate stories, distort the truth, and appeal to
> people's emotions.

3   Read the stories below about alleged German atrocities (cruel
    acts that broke the 'rules' of warfare).

Belgian children were bayoneted by German soldiers in 1914 and their mothers killed.	Germans used corpses of Allied soldiers. The fat was turned into oil and the bones were mixed up with pig food.	German nurses refused to give wounded British prisoners of war drinking water.
Priests in Antwerp, Belgium, who refused to ring church bells to celebrate the Germans taking their town, were hung on the bells.	Innocent women and babies were killed when German warships shelled Hartlepool in 1914.	Over 1,000 civilians were needlessly killed when a U-boat sank the passenger liner, *Lusitania*, in 1915.

4   Imagine you work for the government as a propaganda artist.
    Using a plain sheet of A4 paper, create a propaganda poster to
    be displayed in a British newspaper during the First World War.

5   What other alleged acts of atrocity by the Germans can you
    find?

    _____

    _____

    _____

6   Why do you think the British government was so keen to
    advertise alleged German atrocities?

    _____

    _____

    _____

You will need

A The fighter aces

Look at page 34 in your textbook.

1 Read the information below.

Fighter aces were seen as great heroes by soldiers who saw them involved in spectacular dogfights in the sky. They were idolised at home, where newspapers told exciting stories of their achievements.

Factfile

Captain Albert Ball	**Captain René Fonck**	**Baron Manfred von Richthofen**
• Born August 14, 1896.	• Born March 27, 1894.	• Born May 2, 1892.
• Joined Royal Flying Corps in 1915.	• Joined air service in 1915.	• Joined air service in 1916.
• Shot down 44 enemy aircraft.	• Shot down 75 enemy aircraft.	• Shot down 80 enemy aircraft.
• Idolised by the public.	• Had great talent as a pilot.	• Was an excellent pilot.
• Was a fearless pilot and an excellent marksman.	• Was a superb marksman.	• Was an excellent marksman.
• Won Victoria Cross medal.	• Won Croix de Guerre medal.	• Won Iron Cross medal.
• Killed by crashing behind enemy lines on May 7, 1917.	• Died in June 1953.	• Killed by gunfire on April 21, 1918.

2 a Using the factfile, write some details of each pilot's military achievements on the correct medals below.

German   British   French

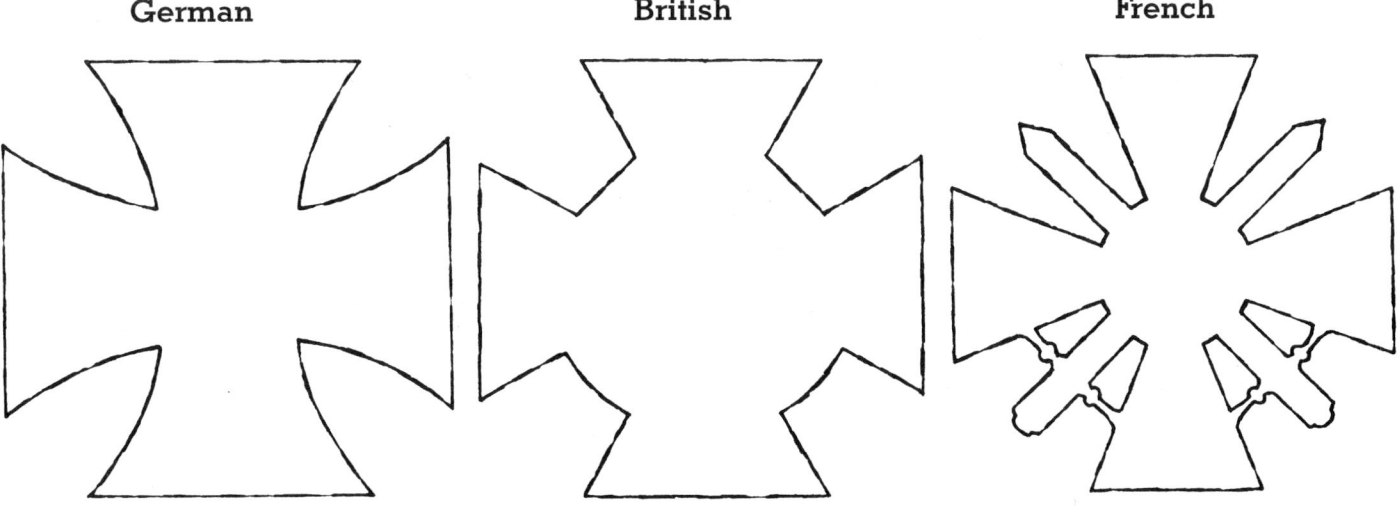

b Fill in the name of each medal on the lines above.

 A *The fighter aces (continued)*

3 Read the information below.

- Many aircraft were made of wood and canvas.
- The cockpits were open and there were no parachutes.
- Pilots had few navigational instruments.
- Aircraft could break up in tight turns.
- On average there were only 50 seconds' worth of bullets per aeroplane.
- Average lifespan of a fighter ace was three weeks.

4 Write two sentences about what could have gone wrong for fighter aces in combat.

_____

_____

5 Look again at the factfile on the first sheet. Write any important personal details of the pilots in the crosses below.

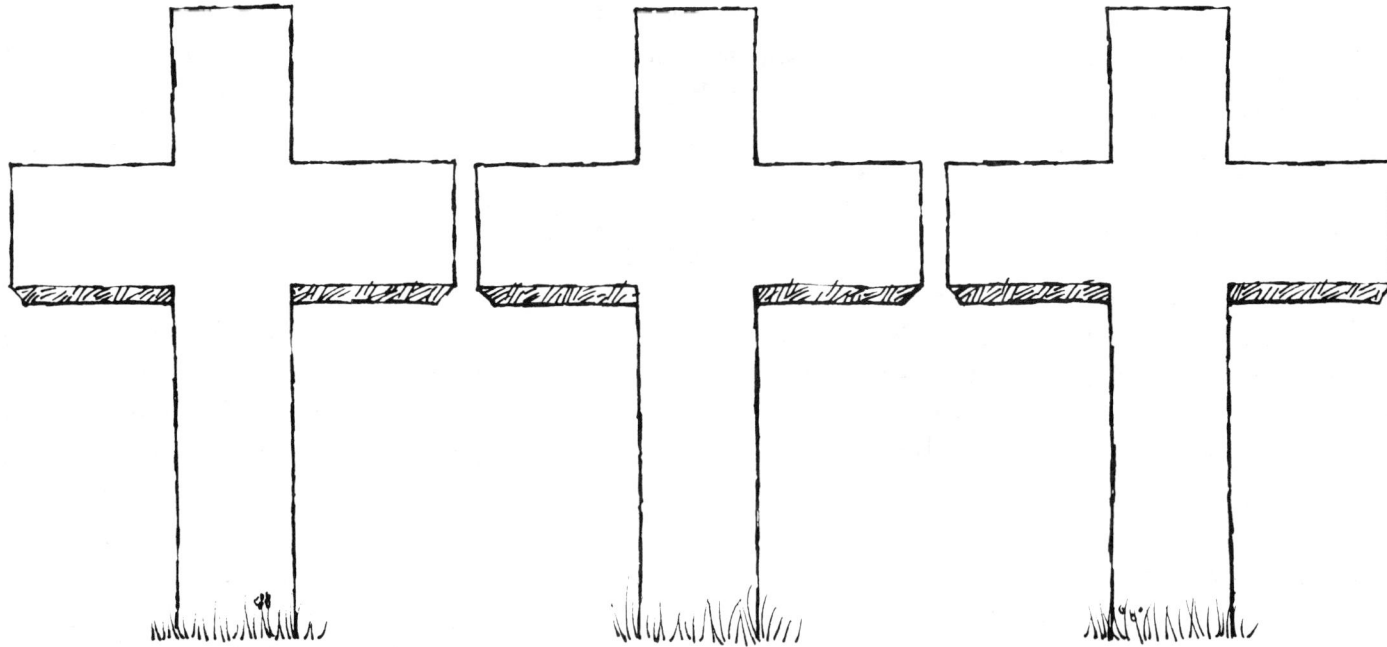

6 Make a judgement: were the lives of fighter aces so great? Explain your answer.

_____

_____

B *The U-boat menace*

Look at pages 33 and 42 in your textbook.

1 Read the information below.

Q-ships were trawlers with hidden guns. Crews pretended to abandon ship when a U-boat surfaced. Then they fired on the U-boat. Some were sunk.

Later, U-boats had a top speed of 14 knots, four torpedo tubes and a gun on deck. They needed a crew of 28 men. They could operate in the Atlantic Ocean and there were normally about 100 U-boats in service at any one time.

Later in the war, more underwater mines were laid between the Orkney Islands and Norway. This minefield contained 69,000 mines and was called 'The Northern Barrage'. It made getting into the Atlantic Ocean more difficult.

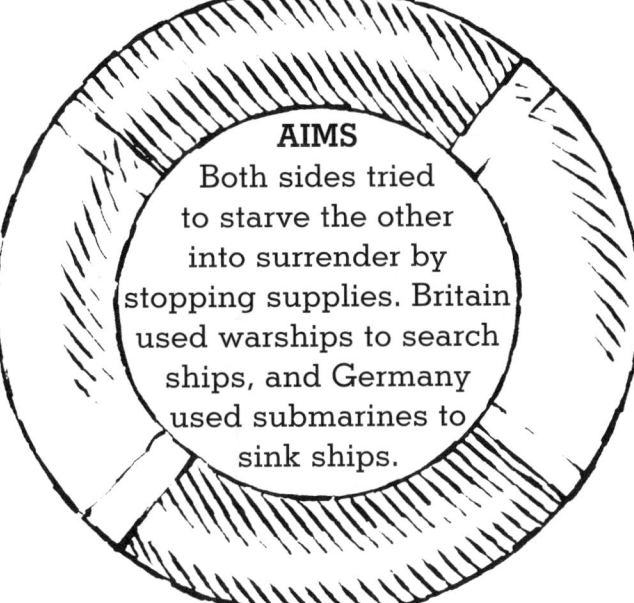

AIMS
Both sides tried to starve the other into surrender by stopping supplies. Britain used warships to search ships, and Germany used submarines to sink ships.

U-boats operated a 'sink on sight' policy to both British and neutral shipping. In 1917 3.4 million tonnes of British shipping was sunk. This left only a few weeks' food supply in Britain.

The idea of 50 merchant ships sailing together protected by 6 warships was introduced in 1917. It was called the 'convoy system'. Warships had echo-sounders and depth charges. In 1918 British shipping losses fell to 1.7 million tonnes. In the years 1917 to 1918 a total of 114 U-boats were sunk.

At first U-boats surfaced when British merchant ships were spotted. The crew were ordered into life-rafts and the ship was sunk by gunfire. However, this tactic was not particularly successful, so British ships were later sunk on sight. The torpedoing of the passenger liner, *Lusitania*, ended the 'sink on sight' policy.

Early U-boats had a top speed of 9 knots, two torpedo tubes and a gun on deck. They needed a crew of 23 men. They could only operate in the North Sea and there were normally only about 25 in service at any one time.

At first underwater mines were laid across the English Channel between Dover and Calais. This was to limit U-boat access to the shipping lanes. A few U-boats were sunk by these mines.

B *The U-boat menace (continued)*

2 Use the information on the previous sheet to fill in details below.

The first U-boat campaign, 1914–1915

Capabilities of the U-boats: _____

_____

U-boat tactics: _____

_____

British solutions: _____

_____

The second U-boat campaign, 1917–1918

Capabilities of the U-boats: _____

_____

U-boat tactics: _____

_____

British solutions: _____

_____

3 Why do you think U-boats had more success in 1917 than in 1915?

_____

_____

4 Why do you think Britain's answers to the U-boat menace worked better in 1918 than in 1915?

_____

_____

_____

_____

 # The Lusitania: what really happened?

Look at page 33 in your textbook.

1 Read the information and sources below and on the next sheet.

The *Lusitania*'s final voyage

The *Lusitania* was a British passenger liner belonging to the Cunard Company. She left New York on May 1, 1915 bound for Liverpool, carrying nearly 2,000 passengers and crew and an assortment of cargo. Between May 6 and 8 the German submarine U-20 was sinking ships off the coast of southern Ireland, on the route to be taken by the *Lusitania*. At 2.12pm on May 8 the *Lusitania* was hit by a torpedo fired by the U-20, resulting in her listing so badly that it was almost impossible to launch lifeboats. At 2.30pm the liner disappeared underwater just after a second explosion.

Source A Adapted from *Lusitania* by C Simpson (Penguin, 1972)

▼

On 19 February 1913 Churchill, 1st Lord of the Admiralty, ordered that the *Lusitania* have... special shell-racking installed, revolving gun-rings mounted on the rear deck... by 8 August 1914 her guns were installed. On 17 September she was registered as an armed auxiliary cruiser. In 1915 the Admiralty ordered British ships to fly the flag of a neutral power... particularly the American flag.

Source B From a letter by Winston Churchill to a government colleague in 1914

▼

We need to entangle neutral ships with the German submarines, and the ships we most need to involve are the Americans.

Source C From a statement by an official of the German Embassy in the USA, May 13, 1915

▼

The sinking was a military necessity not only because she was equipped for fighting, but because we had to protect our brave soldiers from death and destruction by American munitions of war.

Source D From the Mersey Enquiry of July 1915 into the sinking, ordered by the British government

▼

The loss of the ship was due to damage caused by torpedoes. Captain Turner denied that his ship was armed or carrying ammunition.

 C *The Lusitania: what really happened? (continued)*

Source E Adapted from *Lusitania* by C Simpson (Penguin, 1972)
▼

> The U-20 log and torpedo inventory confirm that only one torpedo was fired... the Admiralty refused to release their records.

Source F Adapted from *The Mystery of the Lusitania*, Discovery Channel, 1999
▼

> On May 8, after two days, the Admiralty warned the *Lusitania* of a U-boat in its path. No naval escorts were provided and no change of course was ordered.
>
> A 1993 diving expedition to the wreck of the *Lusitania*, led by Robert Ballard, found the ammunition hold undamaged. He concluded that coal dust ignited by the torpedo caused the second explosion.
>
> Blake Powell, using computer simulation, concluded that cold water rushing into Boiler Room I and meeting with the hot furnace caused a large steam explosion [the second explosion].

2   From Source **A**, what alterations were made to the *Lusitania* between 1913 and 1914?

_____

_____

_____

3   What reasons are given in Source **C** for torpedoing the *Lusitania*?

_____

_____

_____

4   How do Sources **C** and **D** disagree over the ship's cargo?

_____

_____

5   Why do you think Sources **C** and **D** disagree?

_____

_____

C The Lusitania: what really happened? (continued)

6 Source **E** states that only one torpedo was fired. Does Source **D** agree or disagree? Explain your answer.

_____

_____

_____

_____

7 From Sources **A**, **B** and **E**, what do you think may have been the secret motives of the British government?

_____

_____

_____

_____

_____

8 Which source do you think is the most reliable for explaining the mystery of the second explosion? Explain your answer.

_____

_____

_____

_____

9 Look again at all the sources. Do you think the Germans were right to sink the _Lusitania_? Explain your answer.

_____

_____

_____

_____

_____

_____

_____

_____

You will need

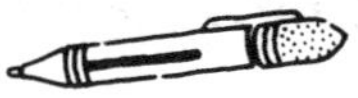

A The fighting

Look at pages 35, 37 and 40 in your textbook.

1 Look at page 35 and read the labels below. Write each label in the correct place on the trench cross-section diagram.

Sandbags • Barbed wire • Dug-out • Duckboards • Firing step
Ammunition shelf • No man's land • Shell crater • Heavy artillery • Machine-gun

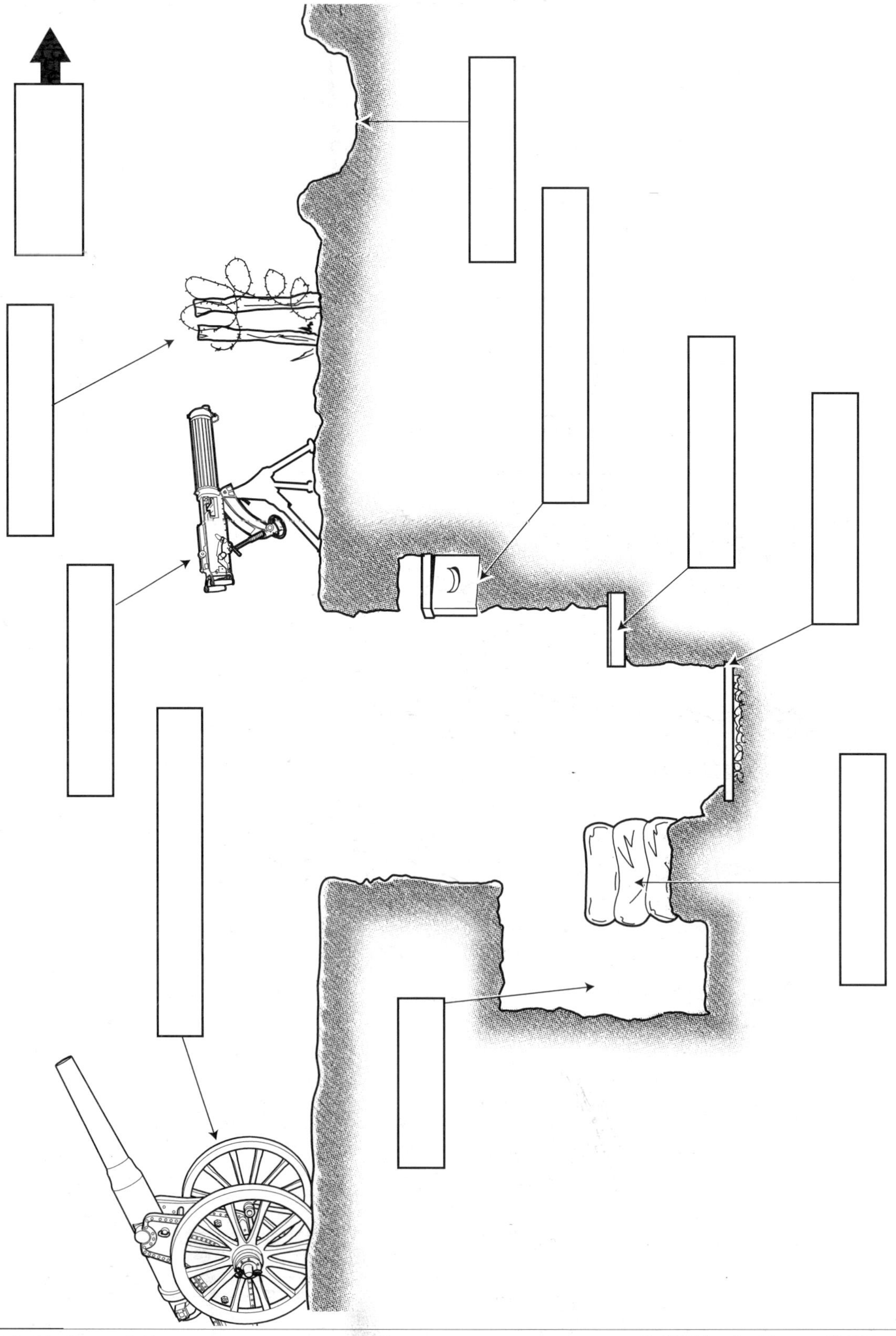

A *The fighting (continued)*

2 Look at page 37. The list of the five steps involved in a major battle have been put in the wrong order. Rearrange the steps into chronological order.

- Bayonets and rifles used if soldiers get near enemy trenches.
- Men go 'over the top'.
- Machine-guns fire on men in no man's land.
- Mines explode under enemy trenches.
- Artillery bombardment.

Correct order

- _____
- _____
- _____
- _____
- _____

3 Look at page 40 to answer the questions below.

a In which battle was poison gas first used?

_____

b In which battle were tanks used for the first time?

_____

c In how many of the battles involving French or British attacks did the Allies make gains?

_____

d Which was the longest battle of the war?

_____

e Which battle had the highest casualties?

_____

f Which battle had the lowest casualties?

_____

A Life in the trenches

Look at page 36 in your textbook.

1 In a normal month, how many days did soldiers spend in the trenches?

_____

2 In a normal month, how many days did soldiers spend away from the trenches?

_____

3 Look below at three of the jobs that soldiers in the trenches had to do. Next to each job write down what weapon or tool you think they would have used.

Sentry duty _____

Trench maintenance _____

Cleaning rifles _____

4 Complete the table below. (Where boxes are shaded means that there is no answer).

Cause	Problem	Solution
	Smell	
	Trench foot	
	Lice on men's bodies	
	Rats	
	Mental torture	

B Deserters and mutineers

Look at page 36 in your textbook.

1 Study the sources below and on the next sheet.

Source A By a recent historian
▼

> The need for orders to be carried out without question was vital to all armies in the First World War. Any soldier refusing to obey an order [mutiny] or running away [desertion] had to be dealt with firmly otherwise thousands of others would have done the same. All countries in the war had to deal with deserters and mutineers, and all took the same solution to the problem.

Source B By a British soldier who served on the Western Front
▼

> At the time I never questioned or was greatly disturbed by what we had to do... I thought that if a man was to be shot for desertion he had done something very wrong and let us down.

Source C By a historian of the First World War
▼

> A court martial was for cases of desertion or mutiny, where the accused often had to defend himself. Judgement was made by army officers, not by juries. Cases often lasted only 20 minutes, and few were found innocent. The normal punishment was death by firing squad.

Source E Death by firing squad
▼

Source D From the recollections of a member of a British firing squad
▼

> There were 12 of us in the firing squad... I did not know which rifles had real ammunition and which had blanks, but all had to be fired at the same time. We had to aim for the heart... stretcher bearers took away each body.

 B **Deserters and mutineers (continued)**

Source F By J Sweeney in the *Observer*, November 14, 1999 (adapted)

▼

> Harry Farr was an experienced soldier who had withstood repeated shelling until he collapsed in May 1915 with 'shell shock' [trembling and frequent nightmares]. Although he returned to duty he soon became unable to fight any more. His request for medical help was refused, and instead was court martialled. He was found guilty and shot at dawn on October 16, 1916. Later at her local post office Gertrude Farr was refused a pension because they were not given to the widows of cowards.

2 From Source **A**, what is meant by 'mutiny' and 'desertion'?

_____

_____

3 Which sources support the view that deserters and mutineers be severely punished? Write a sentence of proof from the sources.

_____

_____

4 What impression do you get from Source **C** about a court martial?

_____

_____

5 From Source **D**, why do you think some rifles contained blanks?

_____

_____

6 Which sources do you think would be useful to someone today who wants to see the 'coward' label removed from deserters and mutineers? Explain your answer.

_____

_____

_____

_____

B Weapons and casualties

Look at pages 37 to 39 in your textbook.

1 Read the information below.

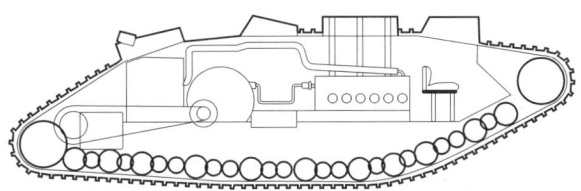

- First used at Battle of the Somme, July 1916.
- Carried five machine-guns and 33,000 rounds of ammunition.
- Crossed no man's land to crush barbed wire, fire on enemy trenches and cross trenches. Men moved behind them.
- 1916–1917: Got stuck in mud, broke down and there were too few.
- 1917–1918: Firm ground and enough tanks – made great advances.
- Killed fewer men than other major weapons.

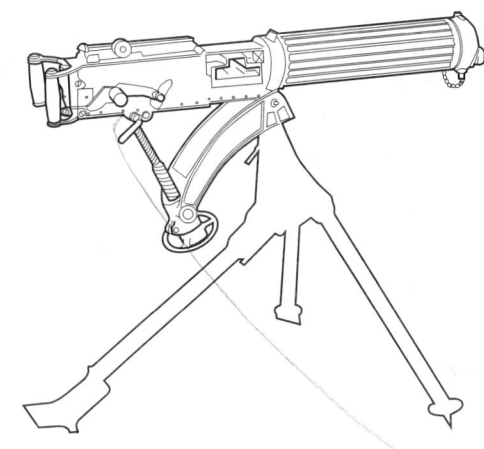

- First used September 1914.
- Fired 600 bullets a minute.
- Used on men advancing across no man's land.
- Second biggest killer – ruled battlefields.

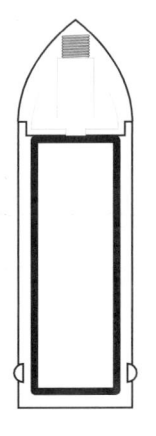

- First used at Ypres, April 1915, in cylinders (chlorine gas).
- Phosgene and mustard gas fired in shells.
- Helped infantry attacks.
- Caused burns to skin and lungs, blindness, and death by choking.
- Gas masks used from 1916, which filtered out poisonous fumes.
- Killed more men than tanks.

- Heavy artillery used from December 1914.
- Fired high-explosive shells and shrapnel shells weighing from 7kg to 1 tonne.
- Used to bombard enemy trenches before big attack.
- Very little protection against shells.
- Deadliest weapon of the war.

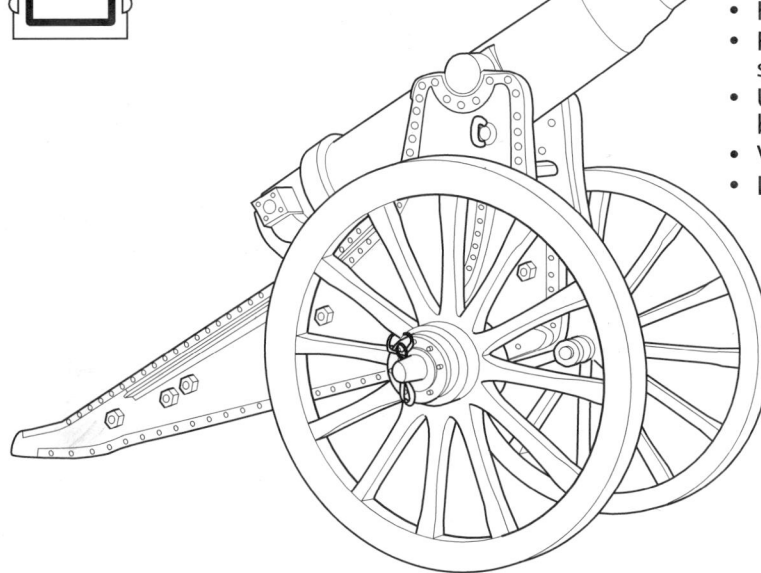

B *Weapons and casualties (continued)*

2   Use the information on the previous sheet to fill in the details on the cross below. Write details of the weapon that caused the most casualties in the largest area, details of the second most deadly weapon in the second largest area, and so on.

①

②

③

① Name of weapon

② Capabilities

③ How used

①
②
③

①
②
③

①

②

③

3   Look again at the previous sheet.

a   Which two weapons helped soldiers to defend trenches?

_____

b   Which two weapons helped soldiers to attack trenches?

_____

 C *Songs and poems*

Look at pages 24, 25 and 36 in your textbook.

1 Read the songs and poems below and on the next sheet. Most songs of the time were not written by soldiers, but sometimes they added their own words to existing tunes. Siegfried Sassoon and Wilfred Owen both fought on the Western Front.

Song A 'Your King and Country Want You'
▼

> Oh, we don't want to lose you,
> But we think you ought to go,
> For your King and your Country
> Both need you so.
> We shall want you and miss you,
> But with all our might and main,
> We shall cheer you, thank you, kiss you,
> When you come back again.

Song B 'It's a Long, Long Way to Tipperary'
▼

> It's a long way to Tipperary,
> It's a long way to go.
> It's a long way to Tipperary,
> To the sweetest girl I know.
> Goodbye Piccadilly,
> Farewell Leicester Square;
> It's a long, long way to Tipperary,
> But my heart's right there.

Song C 'Never Mind'
▼

> If old Jerry shells the trench never mind,
> If old Jerry shells the trench never mind,
> Though the blasted sandbags fly,
> You have only once to die,
> If old Jerry shells the trench never mind.

2 a Using the songs above, complete this table.

Song title	Topic/aspect of war	Attitude of soldiers/country

b What effect do you think singing songs **B** and **C** had on soldiers?

 C *Songs and poems (continued)*

Poem A From *Dulce et Decorum Est* by
Wilfred Owen
▼

> Gas! GAS! Quick, boys! An ecstacy of fumbling,
> Fitting the clumsy helmets just in time,
> But someone still was yelling out and stumbling,
> And flound'ring like a man in fire or lime...
> Dim, through the misty panes and thick green light,
> As under a green sea, I saw him drowning.
> In all my dreams before my helpless sight,
> He plunges at me, guttering, choking, drowning.

Poem C *From Suicide in the Trenches*
by Siegfried Sassoon
▼

> I knew a simple soldier boy
> Who grinned at life in empty joy,
> Slept soundly through the lonesome dark,
> And whistled early with the lark.
>
> In winter trenches, cowed and glum,
> With crumps and lice and lack of rum,
> He put a bullet through his brain.
> No one spoke of him again.

Poem B *The General* by Siegfried Sassoon
▼

> 'Good morning; good morning!', the General said
> When we met him last week on our way to the line.
> Now the soldiers he smiled at are most of 'em dead,
> And we're cursing his staff for incompetent swine.
> 'He's a cheery old card,' grunted Harry to Jack
> As they slogged up to Arras with rifle and pack.
>
> But he did for them both by his plan of attack.

3 a Using the poems above, complete this table.

Name of poet	Topic/aspect of war	Attitude of poet

b Which people do you think Owen and Sassoon hoped would read their poems?

_____

c What message about the war do you think the poets hoped to get across?

_____

You will need

C *Why could neither side win?*

Look at pages 37 to 39 in your textbook.

1 Read the information below.

> The year 1914 saw a 'war of movement' when armies could attack and gain land, for example the German invasion of Belgium and France. What followed for the next three years was trench warfare, in which neither side could win. This is called a 'war of deadlock'.

2 In the boxes below, write relevant details about how four main weapons helped to contribute to the deadlock.

3 Label each weapon as 'For attack' or 'For defence'.

4 In the middle box, write details about how the tactics and leadership helped to contribute to the deadlock.

Weapon 1 _____

_____

_____

_____

_____

Weapon 2 _____

_____

_____

_____

_____

Tactics and leadership

_____

_____

_____

_____

Weapon 3 _____

_____

_____

_____

Weapon 4 _____

_____

_____

_____

C Why could neither side win? (continued)

5 Look again at the top of the previous page at the definition of 'war of movement'. Explain what is meant by the term 'war of deadlock'.

_____

_____

_____

6 On the previous sheet, why do you think the 'Tactics and leadership' box has been drawn in the middle?

_____

_____

_____

7 a On the left in the table below, list other weapons used in trench warfare.
  b On the right, write down any important details of the weapons.

Weapon	Details

8 Look again at the diagram you completed on the previous sheet.
  a Which of the four main weapons do you think caused the greatest number of casualties? Explain your choice.

_____

_____

_____

  b Which of the four main weapons do you think caused the least number of casualties? Explain your choice.

_____

_____

_____

_____

A The end of the war

Look at pages 47 and 48 in your textbook.

1 Cross out the wrong answers in the brackets below, leaving only the correct answers.

a The Kaiser abdicated on
(November 8 / November 9 / November 10).

b Germany's allies – Bulgaria, Turkey and Austria-Hungary –
gave in (before / after) Germany surrendered.

c The Germans signed a (ceasefire / treaty) at 11am on
November 11, 1918.

d The war ended when the Germans surrendered in
(a railway carriage / a tent / an army HQ building).

e The British Prime Minister at the end of the war was
(Asquith / Lloyd George / Churchill).

2 Which of the six nations mentioned suffered most soldiers
killed in the First World War?

_____

3 Which of the six nations mentioned suffered least soldiers
killed?

_____

4 Complete the table below.

Circumstances of death	Message on headstone
Identifiable body	
Unidentifiable body	

5 Where is the tomb of the Unknown Warrior?

_____

6 Which flower is used in services to remember those who lost
their lives in wars?

_____

You will need

B Front-page news

Look at pages 46 and 47 in your textbook. Use the information there to write a front-page report for a British newspaper dated at the end of the war.

- Include the following:
  – the name of the newspaper.
  – the headline.
- Write the story in five parts: US troops, Failure of German attacks, Use of tanks by Allies, Low German morale, Final German surrender.
- Write your article from the winning side – make the Allies look to be the heroes and the Germans the villains.
- Lay out your front-page like the one below.

THE DAILY GLOBE
NOV 12TH. 1918
1D.
THEY THINK IT'S ALL OVER ~ IT IS NOW!
US troops
Failure of German attacks
Use of tanks by Allies
Low German morale
Final German surrender

C Could the war be won?

1 Read the thought bubbles below **before** using your textbook. The thoughts represent the hopes of both sides in early 1918.

(a) We expect about one million US soldiers to fight for our side – they must make a difference.

(b) Huge numbers of new tanks will be available. They are well armed and should be reliable.

(c) I can use 50 whole divisions on the Western Front. These men have been fighting the Russians on the Eastern Front.

(d) We will soon get agreement from all the Entente powers to create one supreme commander. This should remove indecision.

(e) I have to ensure a win before US troops arrive, so we need to attack in the spring and be bold and quick.

(f) I will order bombardment with a mixture of gas and high explosive shells – but just for a short time, so the enemy will be surprised when our storm troops attack their weak points.

(g) We are confident about our new tactic – no artillery bombardment before a troop advance. The enemy will be taken by surprise.

2 Work in pairs. Imagine one of you is Haig and the other is Ludendorff. Choose the thoughts that belong to the military leader you are representing and write the relevant letters in your speech bubble below.

Haig   **Ludendorff**

3 If the deadlock was to be broken, which side does each of you think had the best chance to win? Explain your answer.

_____

_____

_____

 Could the war be won? (continued)

4 Look at pages 47 and 48 in your textbook. Use the information about what actually happened on the Western Front in 1918 to complete the event boxes below. The pupil as Haig should fill in the Allies boxes, and the pupil as Ludendorff should fill in the German boxes. Use the bigger boxes for the most important events and the smaller boxes for the least important events.

Allies

Germans

5 Which of the two leaders – Haig or Ludendorff – had the most accurate views? _____

6 If the years of trench warfare are described as 'deadlock', how would you describe the style of fighting in 1918 on the Western Front?

_____

_____

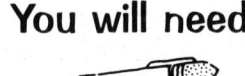

B 'The Good Samaritan of Gallipoli'

Factfile

Private John Simpson Kirkpatrick

John was born at South Shields in County Durham in 1892. As a boy he looked after the donkeys that gave rides to children on the local beach. In 1909 he joined the merchant navy, serving on ships based in Australia. When war broke out he jumped ship and enlisted in the 3rd Field Ambulance as a stretcher bearer. He dropped the name Kirkpatrick, fearing he could be jailed for deserting his ship.

John landed on the Gallipoli Peninsula as part of the massive Anzac assault on April 25, 1915. On April 26 he found a donkey wandering on the beach and used it to rescue two wounded comrades. As a result, he was allowed to rescue soldiers when he wanted, as long as he reported to the field hospital once a day.

Normally he worked during day and night leading his donkey through Shrapnel and Monash Gullies to Quinn's Post. There he left the donkey and crawled through dense scrub until he saw a wounded soldier. Then he ran to

Private Kirkpatrick

the man and put him over his shoulder before running back to cover. The wounded soldier was put on the donkey and led back to the casualty clearing station on the beach.

John did this for 24 days, never fearing death nor being held back by Turkish machine-gun fire. Anzac soldiers in their trenches usually stared in disbelief at 'the man with the donkey'.

On May 19, 1915 John set off to rescue more soldiers, telling his comrades to have a good dinner ready for him. This time he did not return, having been shot through the heart by a machine-gun bullet. He had rescued over 300 soldiers in just 24 days, and had earned the nickname 'the Good Samaritan of Gallipoli'. His body was buried at Hell Spit on the day of his death. Attempts were made for John to be awarded a posthumous Victoria Cross medal, but this was refused. Was he the bravest man never to win a VC?

Adapted from *The Man with the Donkey* by Sir Irving Benson (Hodder and Stoughton, 1965)

You will need

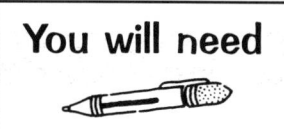

B 'The Good Samaritan of Gallipoli' (continued)

Use the information on the previous sheet to write a suitable epitaph for John Simpson Kirkpatrick on the headstone below. You may wish to include some of these details:

- 202 Private John Simpson Kirkpatrick.
- Australian Army Medical Corps.
- Died May 19, 1915, aged 22.

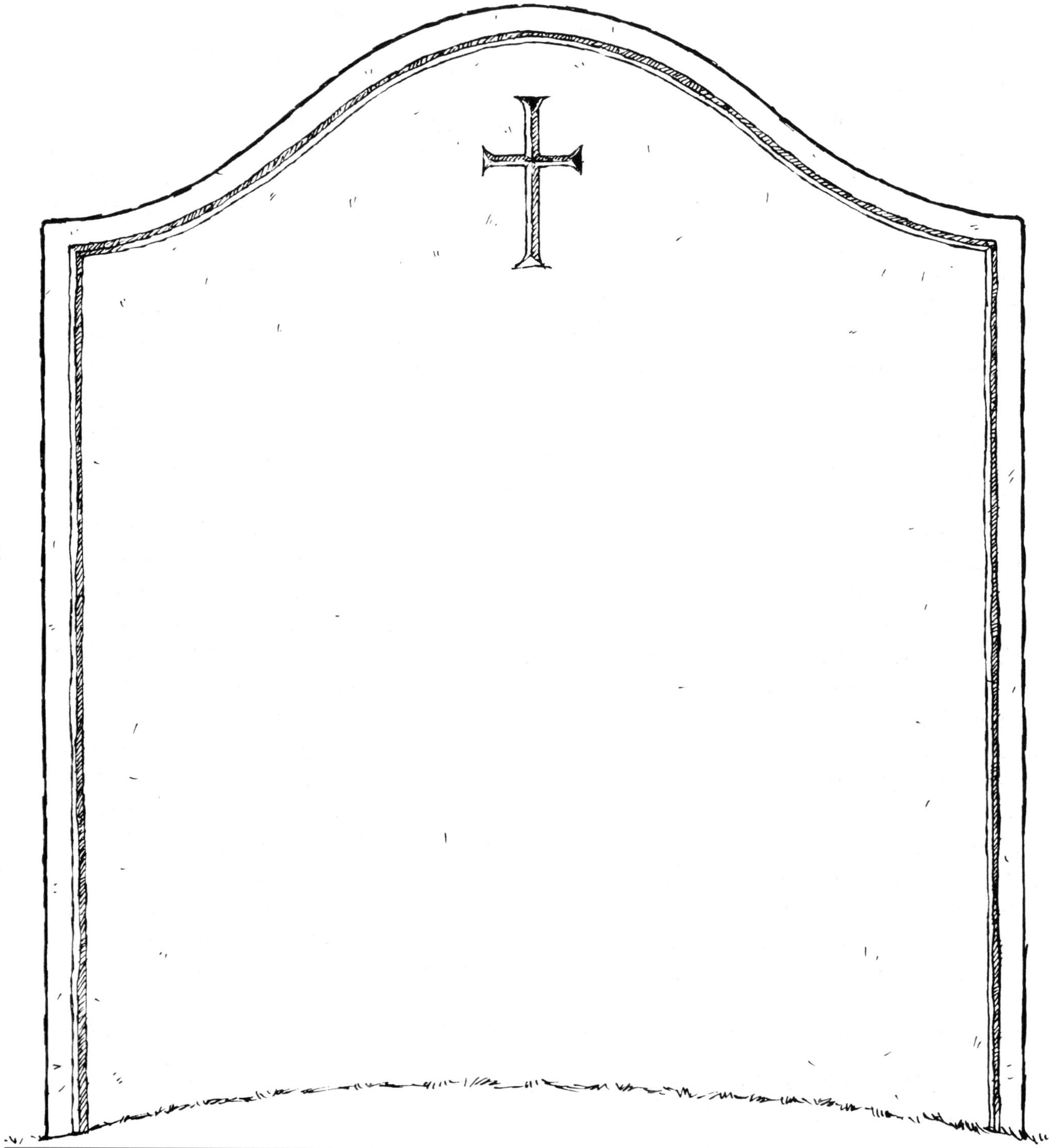

C *'I'll get 50 Germans for that'*

Factfile

Sergeant Hugh Cairns VC

Hugh was born at Ashington, Northumberland in 1896 and at the age of 15 emigrated to Canada with his family. In 1915 he and his brother Albert joined the 46th Battalion of the South Saskatchewan Regiment and soon found themselves on the Western Front. Hugh won the Distinguished Conduct medal for his bravery at Vimy Ridge, but sadly Albert died of wounds sustained in fighting on the Drocourt–Queant trench lines. Hugh was extremely upset – the brothers had been inseparable – and so he vowed to kill 50 Germans in revenge.

His opportunity came in 1918 when his battalion were ordered to capture Valciennes, a German stronghold on the Hermann trench line. At the end of October the 46th Battalion managed to take Marley, despite being at only half strength. On November 1, Hugh was ordered to lead his platoon on a scouting mission to assess German defences surrounding Valciennes. When they came under fire he grabbed a lewis gun and rushed the German machine-gun post, killing five Germans and capturing the gun.

When fired on from another machine-gun post, Hugh did the same. This time he killed 12 Germans and captured 18 others, together with their two machine-guns. However, in the action he received a bullet wound in the shoulder. Later Hugh discovered a courtyard containing about 60 German soldiers. With Lieutenant McCloud and three privates Hugh led an assault, opening up with his lewis gun and killing more Germans. They then dropped their weapons and their officer approached Hugh as if to surrender. However, he took out a gun and shot Hugh through the body. Despite falling to his knees, he managed to kill the officer.

The firing began again with Hugh adding to his total, despite being hit by two more bullets. He was hit again after being put on a stretcher. Hugh Cairns died on November 2 of his wounds. He was aged only 21. He had achieved his target of killing 50 Germans, so avenging his brother's death. Later he was awarded a posthumous Victoria Cross medal.

Adapted from *The Suicide Battalion* by J McWilliams and R Steel (Vanwell Publishing, Ontario, 1990)

C | *'I'll get 50 Germans for that'* (continued)

Imagine you are Hugh Cairns' commanding officer. Write a letter to the War Office recommending him for a posthumous medal.

To the War Office,
London

Address _____

_____

_____

Date _____

Dear_____ ,

_____

_____

_____

_____

_____

_____

_____

_____

_____

_____

_____

_____

Yours _____ ,

_____

You will need

 *Research your family*

See if you can find out what happened to your ancestors in the First World War. Here are some ways to find out:

- Ask members of your family – there may be photographs, letters, diaries, etc.
- Visit your local library or Public Record Office.
- Contact the following organisations, either by post or using a computer linked to the Internet:
  - the Army Records Centre, MOD, CS(RM)2B, Bourne Avenue, Hayes, Middlesex UB3 1RF.
  - the Commonwealth War Graves Commission (www.cwgc.org/).
  - the Imperial War Museum, Lambeth Road, London SE1 6HZ (www.iwm.org.uk/).
  - the Public Record Office, Ruskin Avenue, Kew, Surrey TW9 4DU (www.pro.gov.uk/).
  - the Royal British Legion (www.britishlegion.org.uk/).

Name	
Date of birth	
Names of close family members	
Education/childhood	
Job/career	

You will need

Research your family (continued)

Marriage/family

War service

    Regiment

    Rank

    Combat record

Injuries/death

You will need

A The Treaty of Versailles: what the Germans lost

Look at page 51 in your textbook.

1 Study the map below. Four pieces of land taken from Germany
   in the Treaty of Versailles have been drawn surrounded by a
   dotted line on the map. Find these four areas on the map and,
   using one colour, colour them in.

NORWAY

SWEDEN

ESTONIA

LATVIA

——— National boundaries

- - - - Land taken from Germany
       by the Treaty of Versailles

DENMARK

LITHUANIA

North Sea

EAST
PRUSSIA
(GERMANY)

NETHERLANDS

GERMANY

POLAND

BELGIUM

Rhineland

FRANCE

CZECHOSLOVAKIA

SWITZERLAND

AUSTRIA

HUNGARY

You will need

A The Treaty of Versailles: what the Germans lost (continued)

2 Complete the table below.

Land	Country gaining land

3 Look at the pictures below. Pictures **A** and **B** are about different terms of the Treaty of Versailles. Picture **C** is about German views on the Treaty.

   a Use the information on page 51 to help you to write a sentence to explain Pictures **A** and **B**.

Ⓐ

Ⓑ

_____

_____

_____

_____

_____

_____

   b Use the information on page 52 to help you to write a sentence to explain Picture **C**.

Ⓒ

_____

_____

 A *Did the League of Nations succeed?*

Look at pages 54 and 105 in your textbook.

1 The League of Nations existed from 1920 to 1946. Write in the names of member countries in the table below.

Member all of the time	Members some of the time	Never a member

2 The main task of the League of Nations was to keep the peace. Write in the names of the disputes and the countries that gained from each dispute in the table below.

Disputes the League solved	Name of country that gained	Disputes the League failed to solve	Name of country that gained

3 Cross out the wrong answers in the brackets below, leaving only the correct answers.

a When the League settled disputes successfully, the (attacking nations gained / defending nations gained / both nations shared gains).

b When the League failed to settle disputes, the (attacking / defending) nations gained.

c The League settled more disputes successfully in the (1920s / 1930s).

d The League failed to settle most disputes in the (1920s / 1930s).

B What did the Treaty of Versailles mean to Germany?

Look at pages 51 and 52 in your textbook.

1 Use the information concerning German losses in the Treaty of Versailles to complete the three circles below. Make sure you write the details about Circle **C** that affected Circle **B** in the area where these circles overlap.

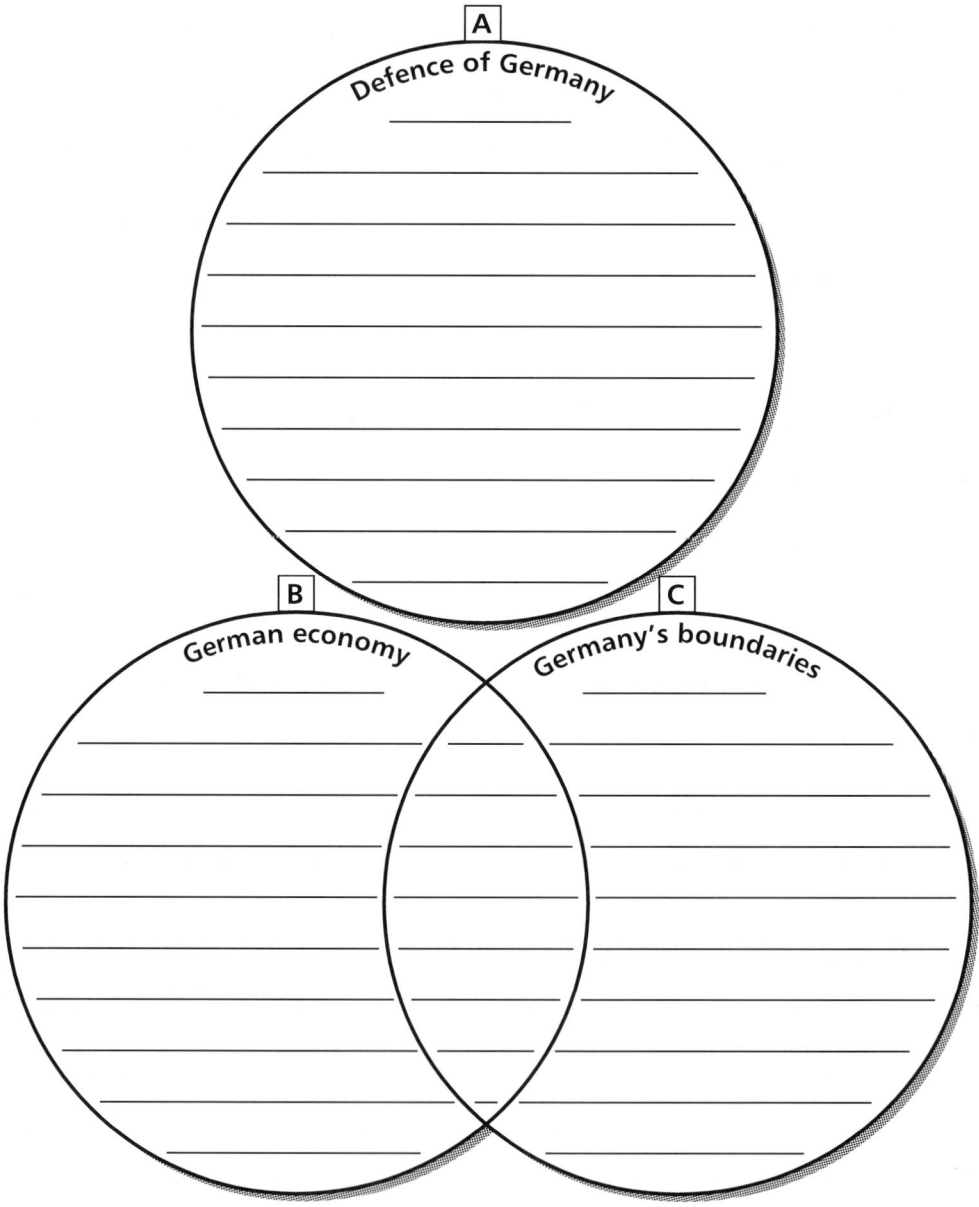

A
Defence of Germany

B
German economy

C
Germany's boundaries

2 Look again at what you have written where Circles **B** and **C** overlap. Why did some areas of land lost by Germany affect its economy?

_____

_____

B *What did the Treaty of Versailles mean to Germany? (continued)*

3 Which part (clause) of the Treaty caused the most resentment among Germans? Explain your answer.

_____

_____

_____

4 For what reason did many Germans feel their government should not obey the terms of the Treaty of Versailles?

_____

_____

_____

5 Why did many Germans believe that their government would not be able to pay reparations?

_____

_____

6 Which part of the Treaty of Versailles was seen as a huge blow to German pride?

_____

_____

7 Why did Ebert, the new leader of the German government, feel that he was forced to sign the Treaty of Versailles?

_____

_____

_____

8 What problems might German hostility to the Treaty of Versailles have posed for Europe?

_____

_____

_____

 How did the League of Nations try to solve problems?

Look at pages 53, 54 and 105 in your textbook.

1 Read the information below.

---

1 Problems concerning peace-keeping
Disputes between countries could be settled in either of these ways:
• By judgement from the International Court of Justice.
• By an inquiry from the Council of the League.

2 Problems concerning the lives of people in member nations
These were referred to the appropriate commission or committee.

| Problems to solve |

Russia is suffering from a serious typhus epidemic. There is an urgent need to improve the supply of drugs to contain the epidemic before it spreads across Europe.

Over one million Greek people living in Asia Minor and Eastern Thrace are homeless and under Turkish rule. Decisions have to be made about where they will live in the future.

Greece has invaded Bulgaria and seized land. As a result, the Bulgarian appeal has just reached the League. It needs to be dealt with urgently.

Trouble between Jews and Arabs in Palestine has flared up again. Britain does not seem to be able to resolve the problem. The League needs to look carefully at Britain's annual report on its rule in Palestine.

Germany and Austria want a free trade agreement between them to help minimise problems caused by the Depression. France has just objected, claiming the plan breaks the terms of the Treaty of Versailles. A judgement will have to be made.

Workers in several member nations suffer from low pay and long working hours. They want to form trade unions. The League has been asked to help.

B How did the League of Nations try to solve problems? (continued)

2   Use the information on the previous sheet to complete the table below.

Details of the problem	Which part of the League's organisation would deal with the problem?	State whether the problem was social, economic or political

3   Write down any examples of successes experienced by the commissions and committees.

_____

_____

_____

4   Write down any examples of successes experienced by the Council or the International Court of Justice in settling disputes.

_____

_____

_____

5   Write down any examples of failures experienced by the Council or the International Court of Justice in settling disputes.

_____

_____

_____

 The Treaty of Versailles

1 Read the information below **before** using your textbook. It tells you about the different experiences of France, Britain and the USA during the First World War.

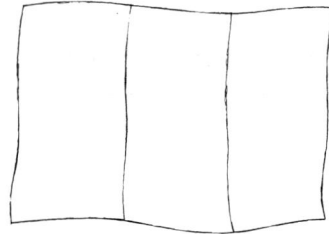

France
- Invaded by Germany in 1870 and 1914.
- 6,000 factories destroyed, thousands of hectares of farmland turned into a wasteland.
- Coal and iron resources used by Germans to make weapons to fire on the French.
- 1.4 million French killed in the war.
- War reduced gold reserves by £25 million.

Britain
- Slight damage to Britain by air raids and naval shelling.
- Lloyd George re-elected by promising to 'hang the Kaiser' and 'squeeze the German lemon until the pips squeak'.
- Lloyd George also knew too harsh a Treaty would not create a lasting peace.
- 1 million British killed in the war.
- War reduced gold reserves by £42 million.

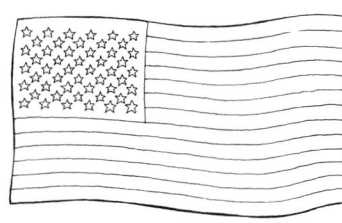

USA
- Fought in the war for less than a year.
- No damage to USA.
- Wilson believed in creating a just peace.
- Wilson lacked knowledge about European politics.
- 126,000 US servicemen killed in the war.
- War increased gold reserves by £279 million.

2 Using the information above, write down what you think each of the three nations' attitudes and demands were to making peace with Germany. The first one has been done for you.

Nation	Attitude	Demands
France	Revenge	
Britain		
USA		

 The Treaty of Versailles (continued)

3 Look at pages 50 to 52 in your textbook.
  a Complete the table below.

	Terms of Treaty of Versailles that benefitted France and Britain
France	
Britain	

  b Complete the table below.

Terms of the Treaty of Versailles that concerned the Fourteen Points

4 How would you describe the terms of the Treaty of Versailles?

_____

_____

5 Which of the Big Three's views dominated the Treaty?

_____

C Was it worth joining the League of Nations?

Look at pages 54, 55 and 105 in your textbook.

Work in pairs. Imagine the year is 1930. One of you is an important League of Nations diplomat who has to make a speech to a country's parliament to try to persuade them to join the League. The other is a leading politician who has to make a speech to the same country's parliament to persuade them to stay out of the League.

1   Read the information below.

Peace promotion outside the League

1921–1922: By the Washington Naval agreements, the USA, Britain, France and Japan are to reduce the size of the navies in the Pacific Ocean.

1925: By the main Locarno Treaty, Germany accepted that her western boundaries, as established at Versailles, should not be changed. This was signed by Germany, France, Belgium, Britain and Italy.

1928: By the Kellogg-Briand Pact, 65 nations agreed not to use force except in self-defence. The main signatories were the USA, Britain, France, USSR and Germany.

The League's weapons to punish aggressors

1   Article 16 (1920)
  a   *Moral* – use world opinion to condemn aggressor nations.
  b   *Economic* – ensure all League members contributed to a joint armed force to remove aggressor nations from lands seized.

2   Later decisions
  a   By the 1923 Draft Treaty of Mutual Assistance, only League members in the same continent as the dispute need take action against aggressor nations.
  b   By the 1924 Geneva Protocol, member nations involved in disputes **had** to accept arbitration. This was not accepted by League members.

Future problems

It was believed that the Italian fascist dictator Mussolini wanted to seize land in Africa. The Japanese were devising a plan to seize the Chinese province of Manchuria. Many observers in Germany thought it was only a matter of time before Hitler took power with the clear plan to overturn the Treaty of Versailles by taking lands.

 Was it worth joining the League of Nations? (continued)

2 Write down the main ideas you could use **either** to persuade the parliament to join the League **or** to persuade the parliament not to join the League.

a _____

_____

_____

_____

b _____

_____

_____

_____

c _____

_____

_____

_____

d _____

_____

_____

_____

e _____

_____

_____

_____

f _____

_____

_____

_____

2 Compare speeches with your partner. Who has the strongest argument? Briefly explain why.

_____

_____

_____

73

You will need

A Making and spending

Look at pages 57 and 58 in your textbook.

1 The car industry created many new jobs. From the boxes below, choose six jobs that were created as a result of the rise of the car industry. Cut them out and stick them on the conveyor belt on the next sheet.

Tyre manufacturers	Steel workers	Upholsterers
Glassblowers	Component manufacturers	Gardeners
Assembly workers	Paint sprayers	Nurses

2 Think of three more jobs that might result from the manufacture of cars. Draw them in the empty boxes at the end of the conveyor belt.

3 On a clean sheet of paper, design a poster advertising a Tin Lizzie. Explain how people could afford to buy it on hire purchase and how this car would make their lifestyle better.

You will need

A Making and spending (continued)

B Jobs in 1920s America

Look at pages 57 and 58 in your textbook.

Americans were encouraged to buy consumer goods through hire purchase and advertising. A worker in regular, well-paid work helped to make jobs for other workers.

1 Look at the following jobs or industries. Using the words in the Ideas box at the bottom, explain what each one does and what other jobs are created.

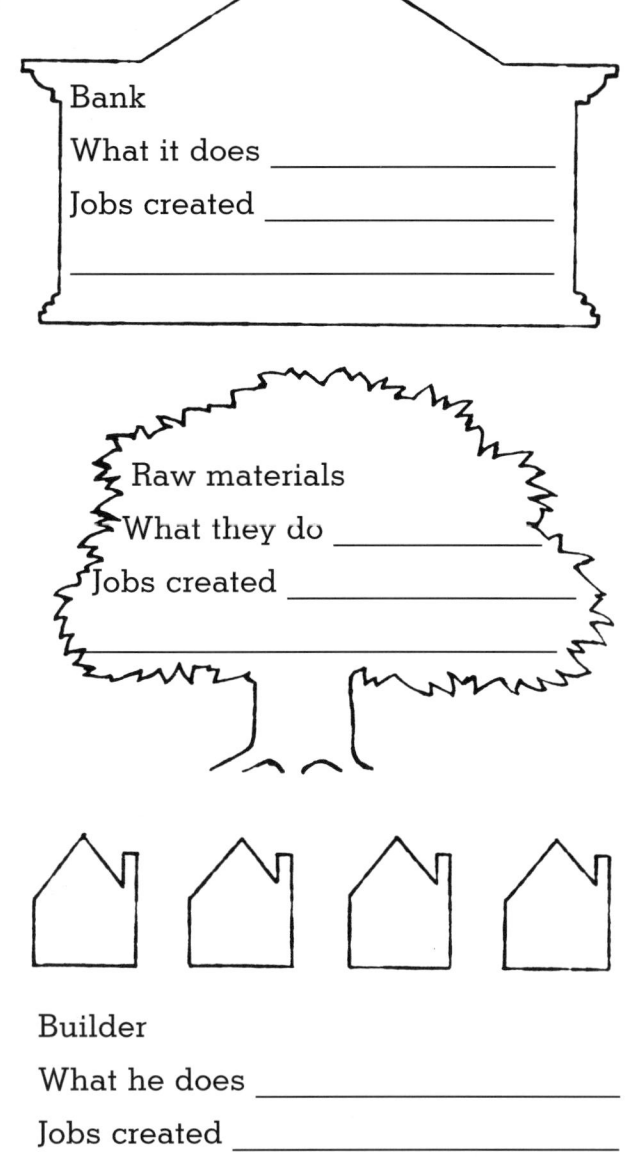

Bank

What it does _____

Jobs created _____

_____

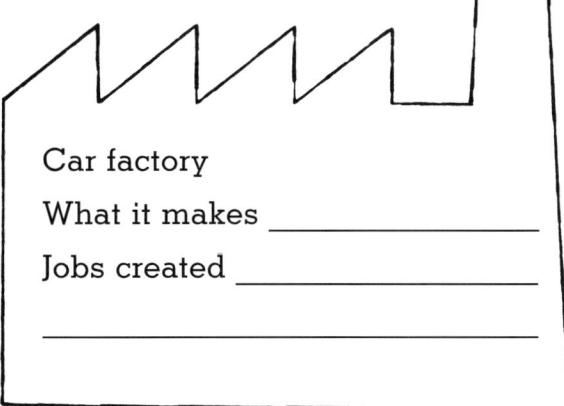

Car factory

What it makes _____

Jobs created _____

_____

Raw materials

What they do _____

Jobs created _____

_____

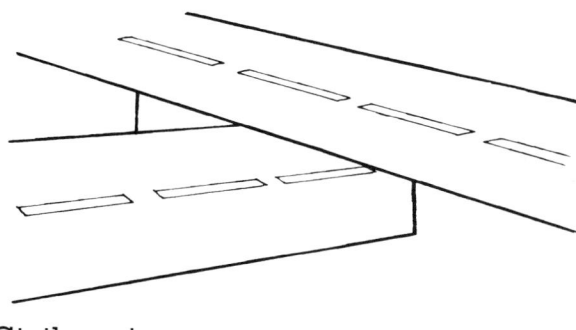

Civil engineer

What he does _____

Jobs created _____

_____

Builder

What he does _____

Jobs created _____

_____

> **Ideas box**
> loans money • bank clerks • timber • accountants • labourers • paint sprayers
> • lorry drivers • carpenters • production works managers • glass makers • electricians
> • brick layers • rubber toolmakers • tyre fitters • oil

B Jobs in 1920s America (continued)

2 The money that people made meant that Americans were wealthier than ever before.

   a Around the dollar sign below, make a list of all the ways that Americans could spend their money.

   b Choose two different colours and underline the domestic (things for the home) spending in one colour and the entertainment spending in the other colour.

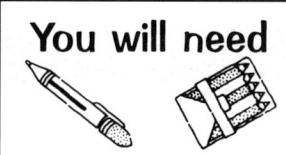

You will need

C Economic boom

Look at pages 57 and 58 in your textbook.

1 The car industry led to the creation of jobs in other industries. On the diagram below, draw coloured arrows between industries where you can see a connection. Use another colour to draw arrows where you can see a connection between industries and consequences for consumers.

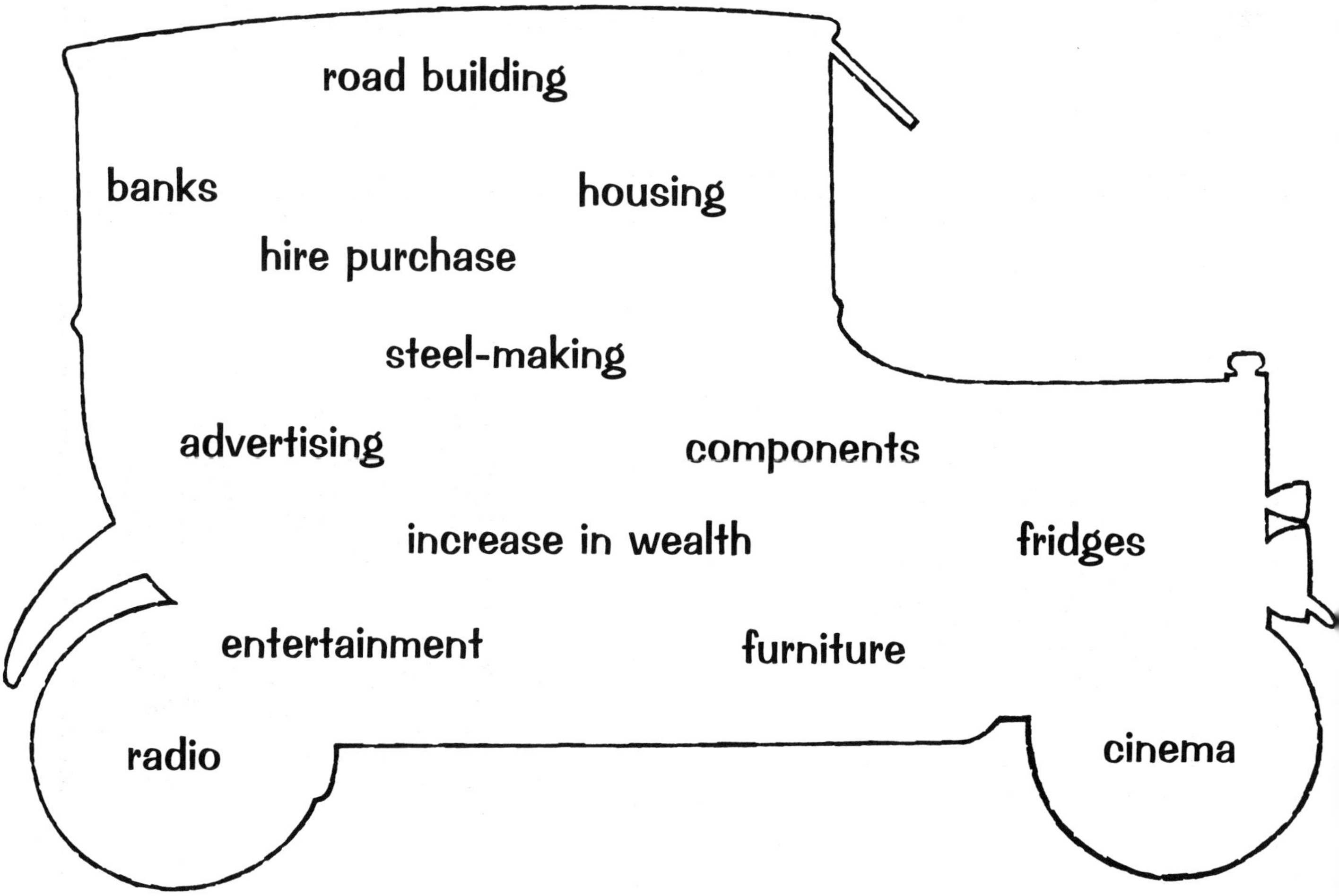
road building
banks
housing
hire purchase
steel-making
advertising
components
increase in wealth
fridges
entertainment
furniture
radio
cinema

2 In 1929 President Hoover said soon there would be '... a chicken in every pot and two cars in every garage'. What do you think he meant by this? Use your connections and consequence diagram to help you to explain how America became so wealthy in the 1920s.

ABC The Roaring Twenties

Look at pages 58 and 59 in your textbook.

Use the following newspaper templates to write your own stories about the Roaring Twenties.

The STARS & STRIPES

PRICE: 1 CENT

DATE:_____

NEW TALKING FILM SENSATION
SILENT FILMS 'OLD FASHIONED' SAY CRITICS

RUDOLF VALENTINO, WHO DIED LAST YEAR, AS HE APPEARED IN 'THE SHEIK'

_____
_____
_____
_____
_____
_____
_____
_____
_____
_____
_____
_____

OUTRAGEOUS!

CHICAGO POLICE ARREST YOUNG WOMEN IN BATHING COSTUMES

_____
_____
_____
_____
_____
_____
_____
_____
_____
_____
_____
_____
_____

REPORTER:_____

ABC The Roaring Twenties (continued)

The STARS & STRIPES

PRICE: 1 CENT

DATE: _____

PUBLIC ENEMY Nº 1

_____

_____

_____

_____

_____

_____

_____

_____

_____

_____

_____

_____

_____

_____

Spirit of St.Louis

THE FLYING FOOL

_____

_____

_____

_____

_____

_____

_____

_____

_____

_____

_____

_____

_____

_____

REPORTER: _____

You will need

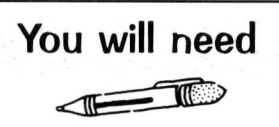

ABC Prohibition and crime

Look at pages 58 and 59 in your textbook.

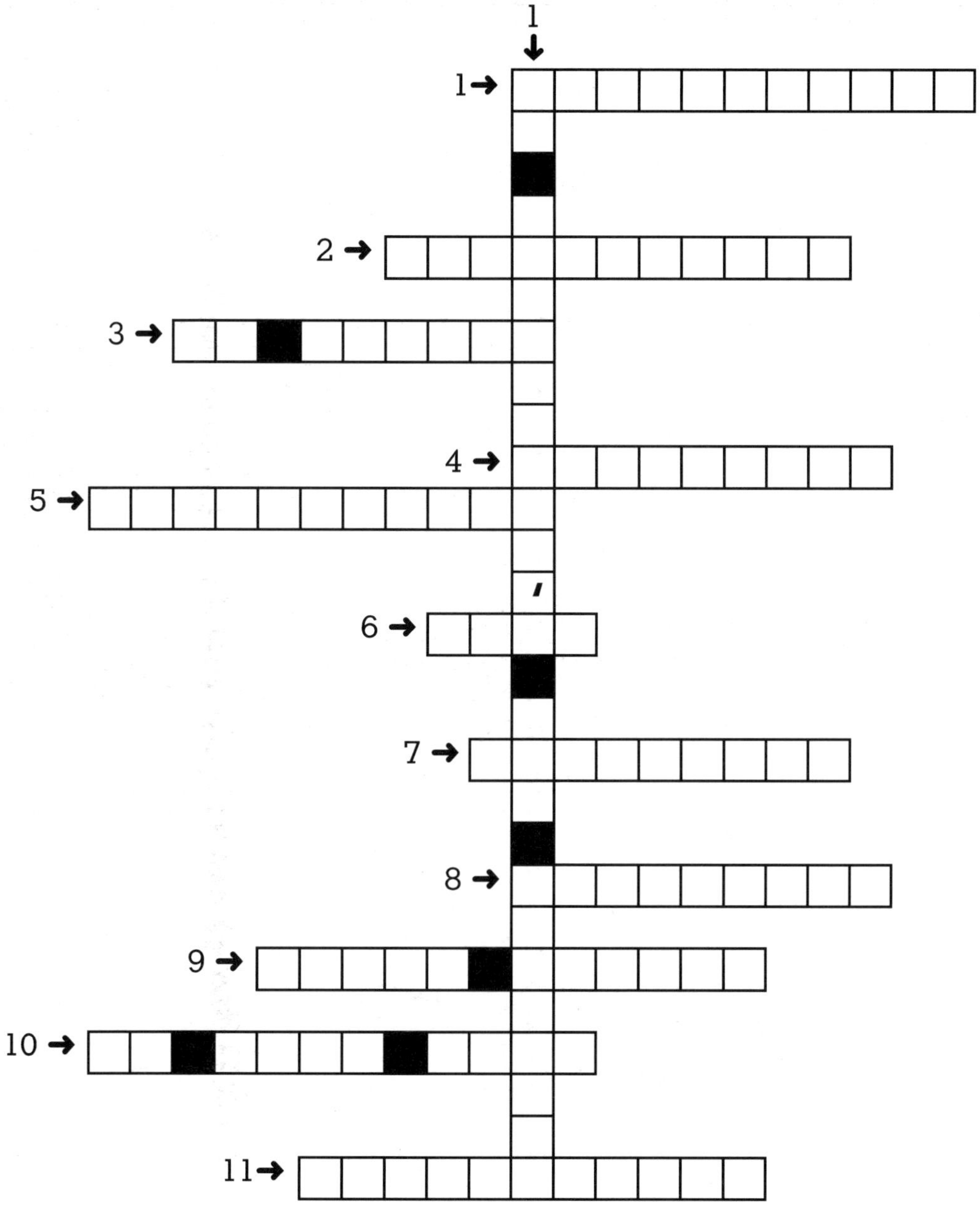

Across

1 Separating blacks and whites.
2 Secret drinking dens.
3 A famous gangster.
4 A foreign-born person.
5 A ban on the sale and transport of alcohol.
6 White Anglo-Saxon Protestant.
7 Criminals.
8 Illegally-made alcohol.
9 The number of immigrants allowed.
10 White supremacists.
11 Smuggling alcohol.

Down

A notorious gangland killing.

You will need

ABC Politics, economics, science and culture

Look at pages 56 to 67 in your textbook.

Copy the words from the Word box into the correct boxes in the diagram. The first four words have been done for you. Some of the words may fit into more than one box.

Word box

lifestyle • law • inventions • business • election • religion • laissez-faire
• electricity • banks • isolation • prosperity • cellophane • cinema • tariffs • flappers
• motor cars • prohibition • voters • companies • depression • music • immigrants
• industry • radio • blues • investors • hire purchase • refrigerator • jazz • shares
• policies • poverty • mass production • bakelite

Words to do with politics

law

Words to do with economics

business

Words to do with science

inventions

Words to do with culture

lifestyle

A Helter-skelter

Look at page 62 in your textbook.

This diagram shows how the Wall Street Crash started. Fill in the important missing words. Use the Word box to help you.

Word box
profits • workers
• demand • money

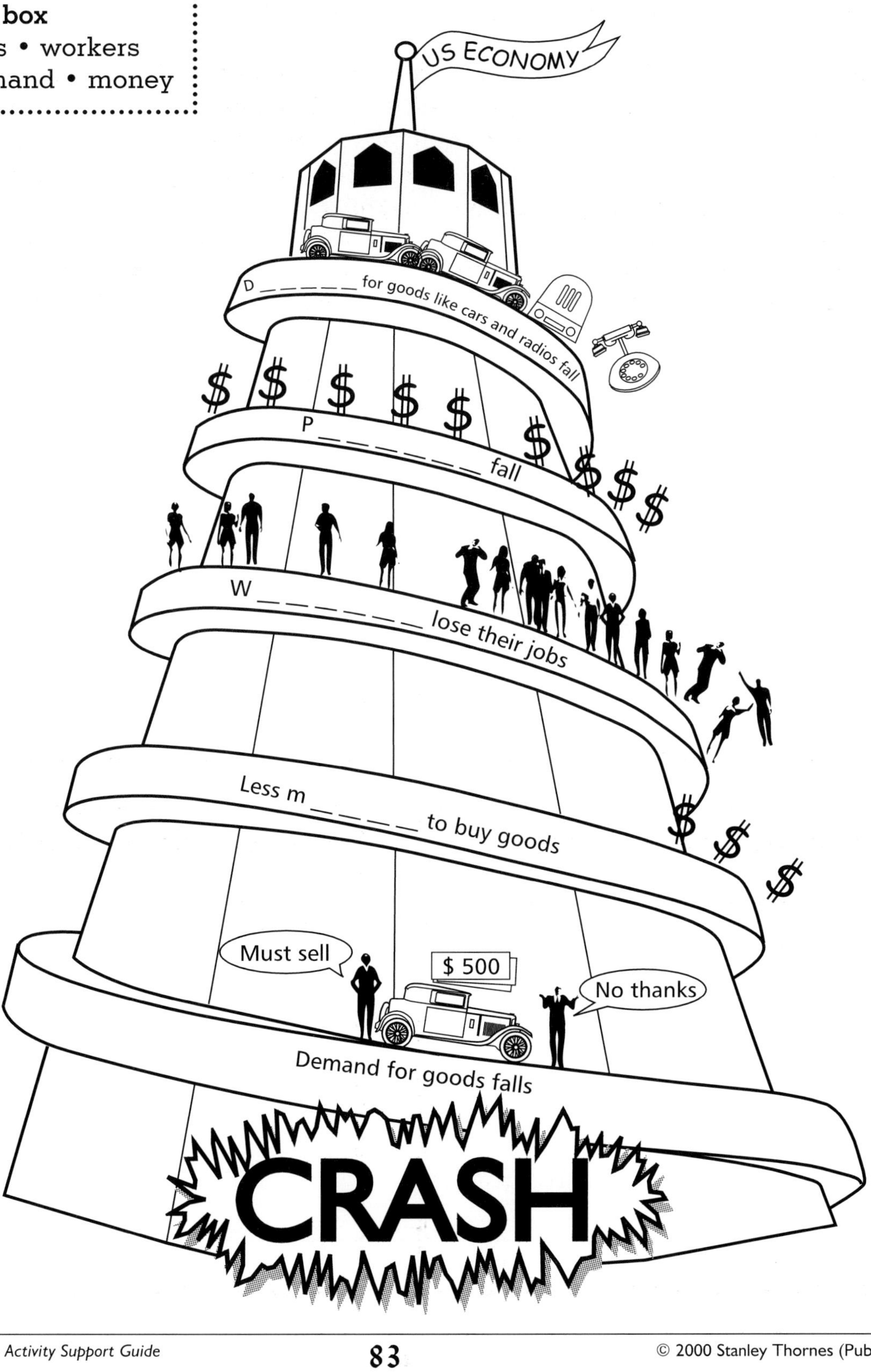

US ECONOMY

D _ _ _ _ _ _ for goods like cars and radios fall

$ $ $ $ $ $ $ $

P _ _ _ _ _ _ fall

W _ _ _ _ _ _ lose their jobs

Less m _ _ _ _ _ to buy goods

Must sell

$ 500

No thanks

Demand for goods falls

CRASH

AB The Great Depression

Look at page 63 in your textbook.

This photograph shows a man who has lost his money in the Wall Street Crash. He owes money to the bank.

1 What sort of job do you think the man in the photo had? (Clue: Look at his clothes and at the car.)

_____

2 Do you think the price he is asking is what the car is really worth?

_____

3 Do you think he will get the price he is asking? Explain your answer.

_____

_____

4 What else might he have to sell to pay off his debts?

_____

_____

5 What might the bank do if he cannot repay his loans and his mortgage?

_____

6 What might his future be?

_____

ABC The Wall Street Crash

Look at pages 61 to 63 in your textbook.

Choose the most likely consequences of six main events leading up to the Wall Street Crash of 1929 by putting ticks in the boxes alongside the correct answers.

1 Some people in America were very rich, but the majority were very poor. Eventually this led to:

a a greater demand for goods like cars and radios.

b a fall in demand and warehouses full of unsold goods.

2 Farmers produced too much food, which:

a meant a fall in food prices so they lost income.

b made Americans eat too much.

3 Farmers borrowed money from banks, but when they could not pay it back:

a the banks threw them off their land.

b the banks loaned them more money.

/ABC/ *The Wall Street Crash (continued)*

4 America found it hard to sell foods to other countries because of the high tariffs, so:

    a she dropped the prices of her goods and tariffs.

    b even more goods were unsold, shops and warehouses stayed full and factory owners laid off workers.

5 Some investors thought that the share prices of some companies were too high, so:

    a they started buying more shares while they were cheap.

    b they started to sell their shares before they got too low to be of value.

6 Investors lost confidence and panic selling of shares started. By October 1929:

    a the Stock Market had completely recovered.

    b parks, businesses and individual investors had lost billions of dollars. Many were completely ruined.

AB Quick quiz

Look at page 63 in your textbook.

1 **a** Who lost money in the Great Depression?

_____

b Why were thousands of Americans evicted from their homes?

_____

c Who was the President of the USA in 1929?

_____

d When was the phrase 'New Deal' first heard?

_____

e Why did the New Deal give hope to many Americans?

_____

f Who promised the New Deal?

_____

2 Write a sentence to briefly explain each of the following words or phrases.
   a Stock market _____

_____

   b Great Depression _____

_____

   c Hoovervilles _____

_____

   d Soup-and-bread kitchens _____

_____

   e Breadlines_____

_____

 **AB** *'Brother, can you spare a dime?'* (1)

Look at pages 62 and 63 in your textbook.

Brother, can you spare a dime? was a song that was written 1932 and was very popular at the time. Here is an extract from it.

> 1 They used to tell me I was building a dream
> 2 And so I followed the mob.
> 3 When there was earth to plow or guns to bear,
> 4 I was always there, right on the job.
>
> 5 They used to tell me I was building a dream
> 6 With peace and glory ahead –
> 7 Why should I be standing in line,
> 8 Just waiting for bread?
>
> 9 Say, don't you remember they called me Al,
> 10 It was Al all the time.
> 11 Why don't you remember, I'm your pal –
> 12 Say, buddy, can you spare a dime?

1 What is his attitude to work and his country in the first verse?

_____

_____

_____

_____

2 What jobs do you think he might have done before the Depression (line 3)?

_____

3 What else had he done for America (line 3)?

_____

4 What had he been expecting to look forward to (line 6)?

_____

5 Why is he now 'standing in line' (line 7)?

_____

6 Why does he have to remind people of his name (verse 3)?

_____

_____

7 Explain why this song was very popular in the 1930s.

_____

_____

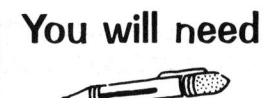

 'Brother, can you spare a dime?' (2)

Look at pages 62 and 63 in your textbook.

Brother, can you spare a dime? was a song that was written 1932 and was very popular at the time. Here is an extract from it.

> Once I built a railroad, I made it run,
> Made it race against time.
> Once I built a railroad, now it's done –
> Brother, can you spare a dime?
>
> Once I built a tower, up to the sun,
> Brick and rivet and lime.
> Once I built a tower, now it's done –
> Brother, can you spare a dime?
>
> Once in khaki suits, gee, we looked swell
> Full of that Yankee-Doodle-de-dum.
> Half a million boots went slogging through hell,
> And I was the kid with the drum.
>
> Say, don't you remember they called me Al,
> It was Al all the time.
> Why don't you remember, I was your pal –
> Say, buddy, can you spare a dime?

1 What is a dime?

_____

_____

_____

2 What jobs do you think 'Al' had done before the Depression?

_____

_____

3 What would he be doing in a khaki suit?

_____

_____

4 Why does he have to remind people of his name?

_____

_____

5 Explain why this song was very popular in the 1930s.

_____

_____

 ## C The Crash: causes and consequences

Look at pages 61 to 63 in your textbook.

Work out what the consequences were for each of the four major causes of the Wall Street Crash. Use the Ideas boxes at the bottom of both sheets to help you, but remember to add your own.

Cause 1: Poverty
Not everyone in America was rich. Only rich people could afford to buy cars, radios, telephones and other luxury goods.

Consequences: _____

_____

_____

_____

_____

_____

_____

Cause 2: Farmers
New machines like tractors helped farmers to grow more food, but they grew too much.

Consequences: _____

_____

_____

_____

_____

_____

_____

_____

Ideas box
demand fell • workers laid off • lots of goods unsold • lower incomes
• warehouses full • borrowed money • unable to repay •
• banks repossessed land • banks called in loans

C The Crash: causes and consequences (continued)

Cause 3: Trade
America protected its own industries by placing tariffs on imported goods. Other countries did the same. American goods were too expensive for people in other countries to buy.

Consequences: _____
_____
_____
_____
_____
_____
_____
_____
_____
_____

Cause 4: Speculation on the Stock Market
People borrowed money 'on the margin'. Companies were valued too high and doubts about the real value of share prices began.

Consequences: _____
_____
_____
_____
_____
_____
_____
_____
_____
_____
_____

Ideas box
investors lost confidence • hard to sell American goods abroad
• share prices of companies that were unable to sell surplus foods fell
• banks demanded repayment of loans • panic selling of shares
• businesses and individuals ruined

You will need

A 'Priming the pump'

Look at pages 64 and 65 in your textbook.

President Roosevelt wanted to create jobs. He called his policy 'priming the pump' because old-fashioned pumps used water to make them pump more water. Roosevelt spent money to create jobs.

In the diagram below:

1 Colour in the boxes where the government spent money in one colour.

2 Colour in the boxes where you think people were starting to go back to work in another colour.

3 Choose a third colour for the boxes where you think the government was making money.

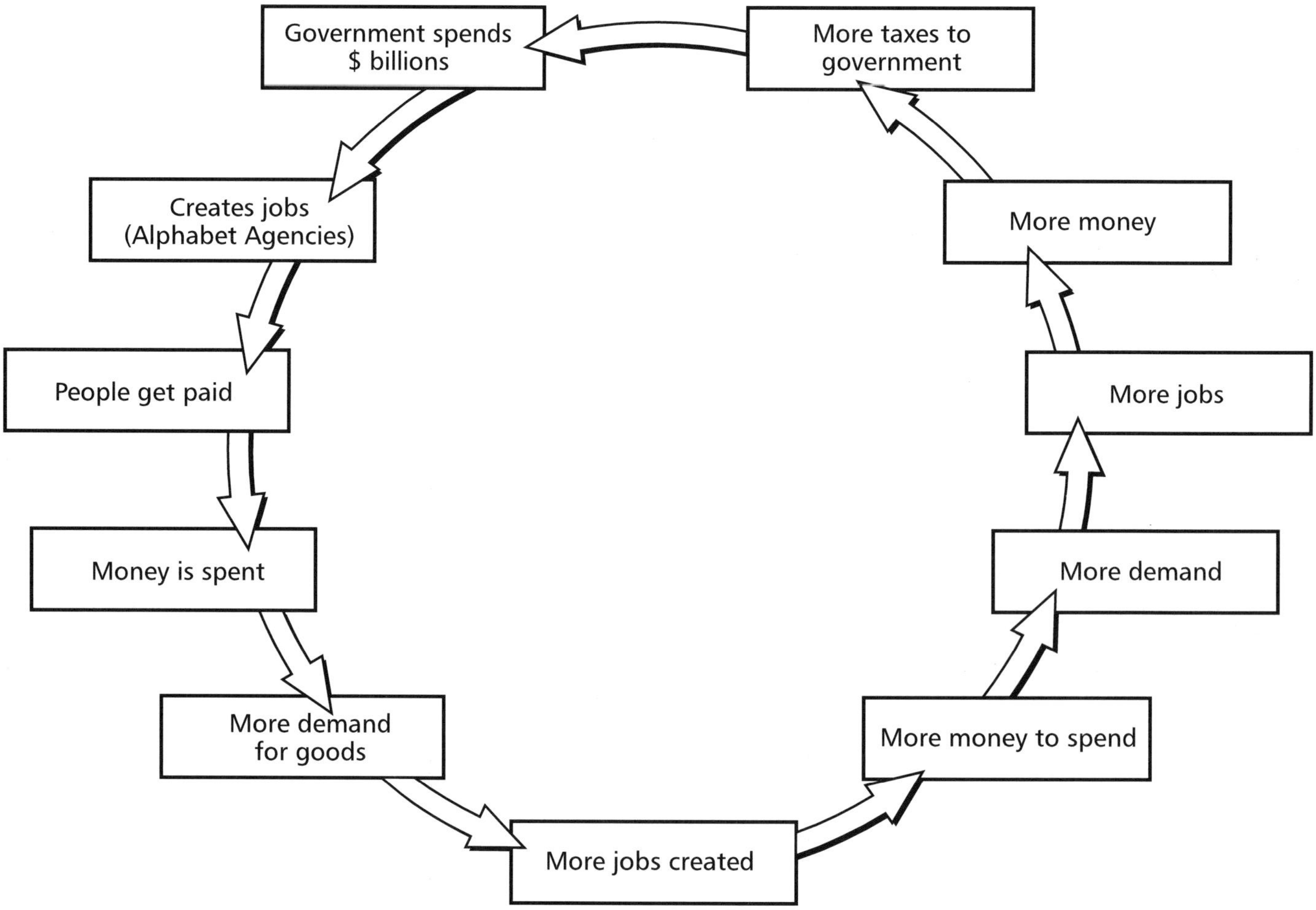

Government spends $ billions

More taxes to government

Creates jobs (Alphabet Agencies)

More money

People get paid

More jobs

Money is spent

More demand

More demand for goods

More money to spend

More jobs created

AB Alphabet Agencies

Look at pages 65 to 67 in your textbook.

Complete the table below about four of the Alphabet Agencies.

Agency	Date set up	Workers helped	What it did
CCC			
TVA			
PWA			
WPA			

 C *Unemployment in 1932*

This source comes from an American government report. Read it carefully before answering the following questions on a separate sheet of paper.

Source A From the *Report of the Government Committee on Unemployment in the United States*, 1932

> During the last three months I have visited some twenty states of this wonderfully rich and beautiful country. At Montana citizens told me of thousands of bushels of wheat left uncut in the fields on account of its low price that hardly paid for its harvesting. In Oregon I saw thousands of bushels of apples rotting in the orchards. Yet there are millions of children who, on account of the poverty of their parents, will not eat one apple this year.
>
> In Oregon the local paper complained about sheep raisers slaughtering their ewes and feeding them to the buzzards because they did not bring in enough at market to pay for their transport costs. Yet in the same month I saw people picking for meat scraps in the garbage cans of New York and Chicago.
>
> In this country we have reached the stage where we have over-production and under-consumption at the same time.

1 Why was wheat left uncut and apples left to rot?

2 Why were farmers slaughtering their ewes?

3 Why were people in cities scavenging for scraps of meat?

4 What does the government report mean by 'over-production and under-consumption'?

5 Which agencies do you think would be able to help the farmers in Oregon and the poor in Chicago?

6 Roosevelt's New Deals were popular with the voters. Give as many reasons as you can to explain why.

7 If you were a young unemployed American in the 1930s:

   a what would you find attractive about Roosevelt's policies? Give your reasons.

   b what might you not like about Roosevelt's policies? Give your reasons.

You will need

Dictionary

 Russian society

Look at pages 68 and 69 in your textbook.

1   Use a dictionary to help you to match up the heads to the tails.
    Draw a line from each word to its meaning.

Heads	Tails
Democracy	A country whose head of state is a king or queen
Monarchy	A country whose head of state is chosen by the people
Republic	A country ruled by a government that has been voted for
Revolution	Someone who has absolute power
Communism	When the government of the country is overthrown
Empire	A belief that everyone is equal
Autocrat	Different peoples/territories under the rule of one person/country

2   Look at the map of Europe in 1919 on page 68 of your
    textbook. Give an example of:

    a a country that was a democracy. _____

    b a country that was a monarchy. _____

    c a country that was a republic. _____

    d a country that was a communist state. _____

3   Using the Word box, fill in the missing words in the paragraph
    below, to describe Russian Society.

    The _____ owned most of the land. The peasants
    were extremely _____. They lived in village
    _____ called _____. The Tsar wanted to
    _____ Russia. Peasants went to the cities to work in
    the _____. The wages were _____ and
    conditions were _____. Businessmen became
    _____ but the workers became _____ and
    their meetings were _____. They felt the
    _____ was not listening to their problems.

    > **Word box**
    > banned • communes • dangerous • factories • low • nobility
    > • poor • modernise • mirs • Tsar • wealthy • unhappy

You will need

A Russian society (continued)

4 **a** Look at this illustration, which is based on a Russian cartoon drawn in 1900.

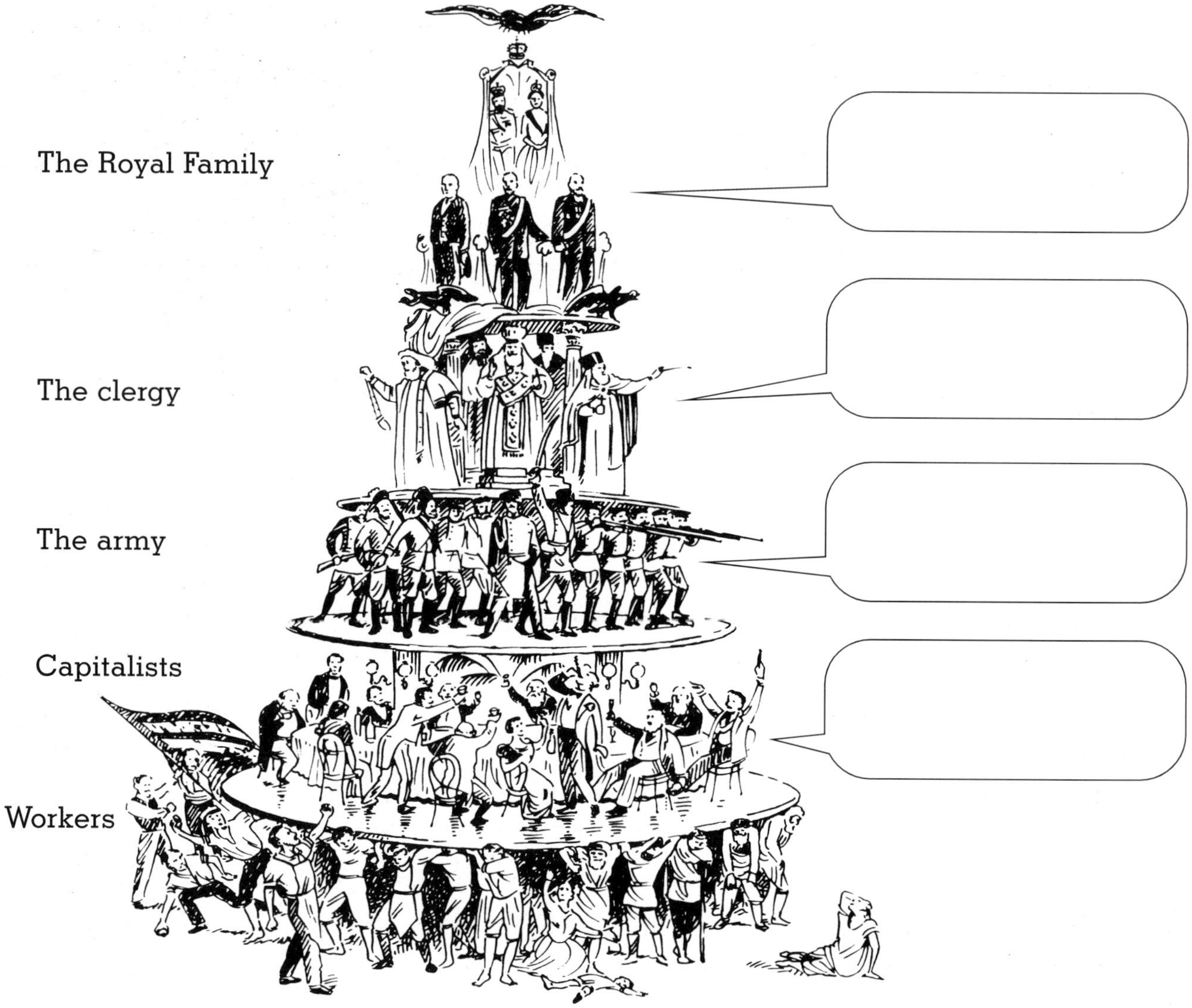

The Royal Family

The clergy

The army

Capitalists

Workers

b Look at the speech bubbles below and, choosing from the top **four** groups in the cartoon, write each speech alongside whichever group you think might have said those words.

We do the eating

We shoot you

We rule you

We mislead you

c Draw a speech bubble alongside the workers. What do you think they might say?

You will need

B Revolution: causes and explanations

Look at pages 69 and 74 in your textbook.

1 Draw lines to match up the causes on the left to the explanations on the right.

Causes   Explanations

| Workers and peasants were very poor |

| Nicholas made poor decisions and tried to rule without the Duma |

| Bloody Sunday, 1905 |

| There were food and fuel shortages |

| Rasputin |

| The people blamed the government for their poverty and decided to rebel |

| The First World War |

| He was hated by many Russians because he led a scandalous life |

| Tsar Nicholas II |

| People blamed the government for the war and the hardships it caused |

| The bad winter of 1916–1917 |

| There was great anger when innocent people were killed so they stopped supporting the Tsar |

| The Tzarina |

| She was distrusted because she was German and was friendly with Rasputin |

2 Choose two different colours. Colour in the **long-term** causes in one colour and the **short-term** causes in the other colour.

 Why was there a Russian Revolution?

Look at pages 69 and 74 in your textbook.

1 Read the information below, which lists some of the causes of the Russian Revolution.

2 What other factors that you think were important? Write them in the box at the bottom of the page.

Workers were very poor. They were often hungry and living conditions were bad.

On Bloody Sunday, soldiers fired on the crowd and 1,000 people were killed.

Rasputin was unpopular. People believed he gave bad advice to the Tsar and led a scandalous life.

During the First World War, soldiers and ordinary people suffered.

Nicholas II could not make decisions and had family problems.

During the bad winter of 1916–1917, there was not enough to eat and no fuel to keep warm.

You will need

C *Why was there a Russian Revolution? (continued)*

3 Using information from your textbook and on the previous sheet, complete the table below. Decide whether each cause was a **long-term** or a **short-term** cause, then consider how important each cause was. Use a 3-point scale: **1** = not important; **2** = important; **3** = very important.

Cause	Short-term cause (tick)	Long-term cause (tick)	Importance (tick)		
			1	2	3

A Bread, peace, land

Look at pages 75 to 77 in your textbook.

Bread, peace, land

This was one of Lenin's slogans.

Which word – bread, peace or land – would these Russians most like to hear? Using the ideas in the Ideas box below, finish off their sentences.

I like the idea of _____

_____

_____

_____

I'm hoping for _____

_____

_____

_____

I want _____

_____

_____

_____

....
Ideas box
Bread: hungry, no food
Peace: tired of war, want to go home
Land: need to grow crops, raise animals, feed my family
....

A Reds v Whites

Look at page 78 in your textbook.

1   Fill in the missing words in the sentences below. Choose from either **Red(s)** or **White(s)**.

Troops from Britain, France and the USA helped the

_____ Armies. The _____ promised to help

in the war against Germany. At first, the _____

retreated. The _____ wanted to rescue the Tsar. The

_____ controlled central Russia and the railways.

They could move fast. The _____ had fewer men and

they could not keep in touch with each other. The

_____ Army was well supplied and well disciplined.

The _____ Armies were badly led and the men were

fed up. The _____ Army defeated them.

2   Find out who these soldiers support and write their speeches
    in either the Red Army column or the White Armies column.

I SUPPORT THE TSAR

I WAS CONSCRIPTED IN 1920

I AM A BRITISH SOLDIER

I AM A TSARIST GENERAL

I SUPPORT LENIN

TROTSKY IS MY GENERAL

MY FAMILY ARE HOSTAGES

Red Army	White Armies

B *Did Lenin keep his promises?*

Look at page 77 in your textbook.

1 Complete the table below by putting a tick (✓) if you think Lenin kept his promises, a cross (✗) if you think he broke his promises, or a question mark (**?**) if you think there is not enough evidence to decide.

Lenin promised to:	✓, ✗ or ?
End the war	
Give land to the peasants	
Help the workers	
Hold free elections	
Allow freedom of the press	
Allow the SR in the assembly	

2 Answer Yes or No to the first parts of the following questions, then try to explain why you chose that answer.

Yes No

- Was Lenin a communist? ☐ ☐
- Because _____

_____

- Was Lenin a dictator? ☐ ☐
- Because _____

_____

- Did Lenin make a good peace with Germany? ☐ ☐
- Because _____

_____

- Did Lenin make friends? ☐ ☐
- Because _____

_____

- Did Lenin make enemies? ☐ ☐
- Because _____

_____

B Civil war

Look at page 78 in your textbook.

Use these sentence starters to help you to answer the question:
'How did the Red Army win the civil war?'

1 The White Armies were in a strong position because

_____

2 The Tsar was executed at Ekaturinburg because

_____

3 Although they appeared to be in a weak position, the Reds

_____

4 Communication for the Whites was

_____

5 The Cheka made sure that

_____

_____

6 Trotsky was Commander in Chief for War. He

_____

7 Discipline in the Red Army

_____

_____

8 Morale was

_____

_____

9 Control of Russia by 1921

_____

_____

 C ***Why did Lenin appeal to the Russians?***

Look at pages 75 to 79 in your textbook.

1 Lenin's promises and slogans were aimed at the ordinary people of Russia, and in particular the soldiers, peasants and factory workers. Explain how each slogan would appeal to each group.

Slogan	Group	Reason
Bread, peace, land		
All power to the Soviets		
Hunger does not wait. The peasant uprising does not wait.		

2 How far did Lenin keep his promises? Complete the table below. The first one has been done for you.

Promise	Was it kept?	Popular with	Unpopular with
An end to war	Yes	Soldiers who wanted to come home	Whites, who felt the peace was humiliating

3 On a separate sheet of paper, write a paragraph to answer the following questions.

    a Why did Lenin appeal to the Russians?

    b How far did he keep his promises?

C | *The Russian civil war*

Look at page 78 in your textbook.

1 Complete the table below.

	Reds	Whites
Reasons for fighting		
Positions of strength		
Morale		
Discipline		
Communications		
Significant events		

2 On a separate sheet of paper, write a report on 'The civil war in Russia, 1918–1921'.

ABC *Stalin: good or bad?*

Look at pages 80 to 85 in your textbook.

1 Complete the table below.

Stalin's actions	Good or bad?	Reason
a Stalin made peasants work on collective farms.		
b All tools and animals had to be given to the kolkhoz.		
c The Kulaks resisted. They were sent to workcamps.		
d Five-year plans were introduced. More coal, oil, electricity and steel were produced.		
e New industrial towns were built.		
f The secret police (NKVD) was reorganised and had extensive powers.		
g Pioneers went to work in new industrial towns.		
h Workers enjoyed better healthcare, education and employment.		
i Many leading communists were purged.		
j The Russian Orthodox Church was destroyed.		

2 Use your information to answer the following questions. Use a separate sheet of paper for your answers.

    a Was Stalin a good leader of the Russian people?

    b Why did he appear to be so popular?

A Hitler and the Nazis in the 1920s

1 Look at page 93 in your textbook. Match up the heads on the left to the tails on the right.

Heads   **Tails**

Ex-soldiers supported Hitler because   the Nazis promised no more rapid inflation

Businessmen supported Hitler because   the Nazis promised public works programmes

Middle-class people supported Hitler because the Nazis promised to re-arm Germany

Unemployed people supported Hitler because   the Nazis promised to let them keep their factories

2 Look at page 91 in your textbook. Name two groups of people who opposed Hitler.

a _____ b _____

3 Look at page 92 in your textbook. Complete the following paragraph about Hitler's views concerning Germany by filling in the missing words.

In 1924–1925 Hitler wrote a book called _____
_____. It contained many ideas; for example, the
Treaty of _____ should be ended, Germany should be
led by a _____, and Germans belonged to the
_____ race of people and all other races were
_____. If he became ruler of Germany, he would
make sure that Germany took _____ from other
countries. A lot of people liked these ideas and so membership
of the Nazi party increased from _____ in 1925 to
_____ by 1931. The Wall Street Crash, which led to
millions of Germans losing their _____, did much to
put Hitler in power as ruler of Germany.

A | Adults in Nazi Germany

1 Look at page 100 in your textbook.

Cross out the wrong answers in the brackets below, leaving only the correct answers.

a Women were (allowed / not allowed) to join the armed forces.

b Women were (allowed / not allowed) to be lawyers.

c Women were expected to (be at home / go to work).

d Motherhood was celebrated in (TV / video / radio broadcasts).

e The Gold Honour Cross Medal was awarded to women with (5 / 8 / 10) children.

2 Look at page 101 in your textbook.

a Use the information there to complete the table below.

The good things for workers	The bad things for workers

b Look again at your completed table and try to make a judgement. You will have written much more in one of the columns than in the other. Explain why.

_____

_____

You will need

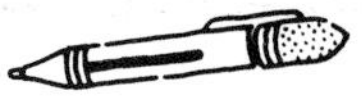

B Hitler's road to power

Look at pages 91 to 93 in your textbook.

1 a Write the following event labels in the correct boxes in the diagram below. Make sure they are written in chronological order.

Relaunch of Nazi party | Mass rallies held | Wall Street Crash | Hitler writes *Mein Kampf* | French invasion of Rühr and Munich Putsch

b Using your textbook, complete the boxes with relevant details about each event that might have helped to make Hitler Chancellor of Germany.

Event label:

Event label:

Event label:

Event label:

Event label:

January 1933: Hitler becomes Chancellor (Prime Minister) of Germany

B Hitler's road to power (continued)

2 Which events do you think helped to make Hitler ruler of Germany?

_____

_____

_____

3 Select any three groups of people who supported Hitler, and for each say why they supported him.

Supporters	Reasons

4 a What method do you think Hitler used to try to become ruler of Germany in 1923?

_____

b What method do you think Hitler used to try to become ruler of Germany after 1923?

_____

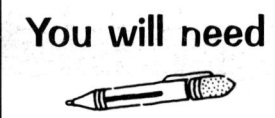

You will need

B Persecution by the Nazis

Look at pages 96 to 98 in your textbook.

1 Complete the diagram below by selecting information about how the Jews were treated by the Nazis. Make sure your answer matches the appropriate year.

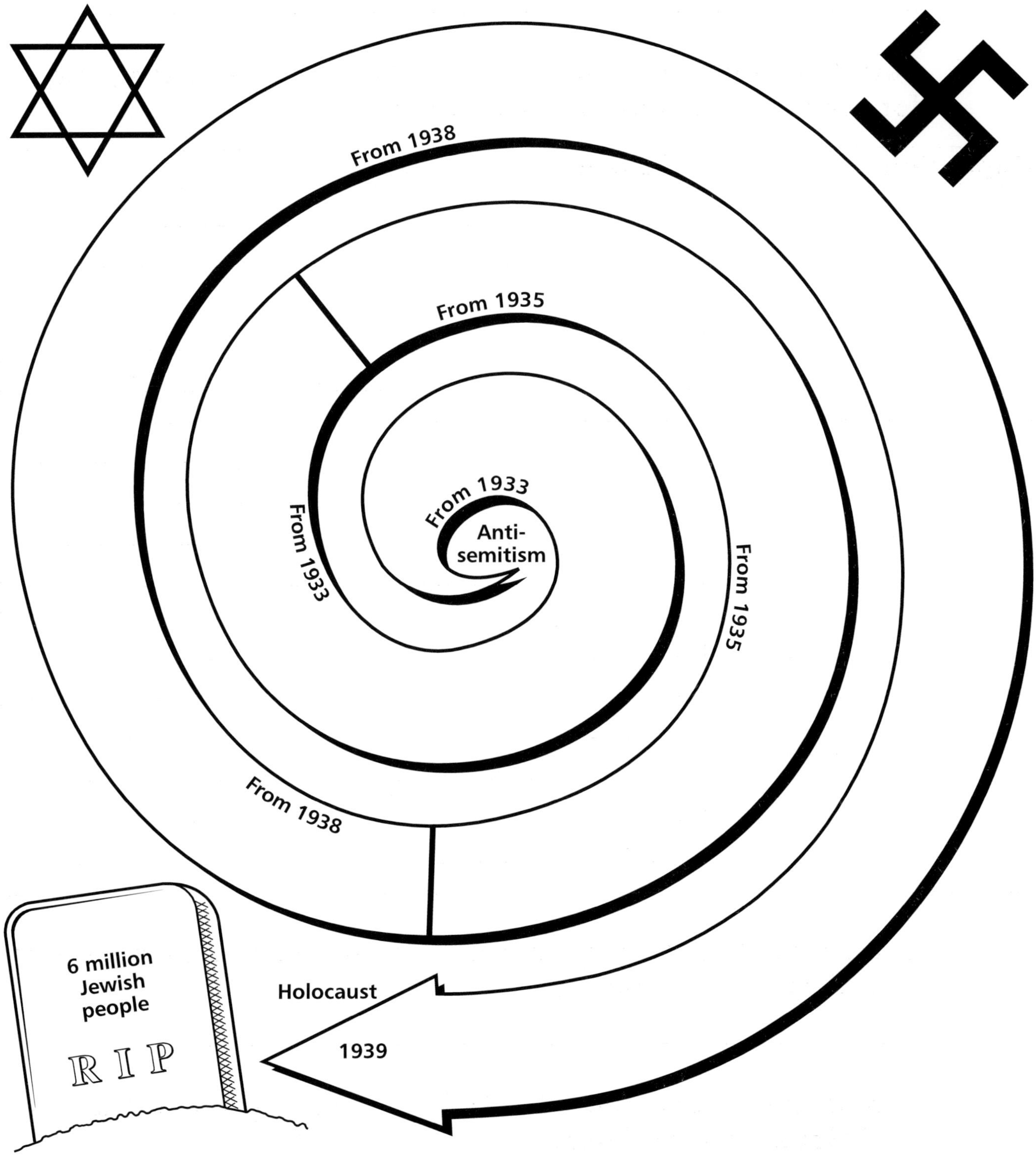
From 1938
From 1935
From 1933
Anti-
semitism
From 1933
From 1935
From 1938
Holocaust
1939
6 million
Jewish
people
RIP

B Persecution by the Nazis (continued)

2 Write down any one reason why you think the Nazis persecuted Jews in Europe.

_____

3 Complete the table below.

Name of group	How they were persecuted	Year persecution began
Social undesirables		
Gypsies		
Mentally ill		
Mentally handicapped babies and children		
Adults with hereditary (inherited) diseases		

4 What changes were made in German schools to:

a textbooks?

_____

b subjects?

_____

5 Look again at your answer to Question 4. Write down any one reason why you think the Nazis made changes in schools.

_____

C How Hitler became the German leader

Look at pages 91 to 93 in your textbook.

1 Read the information below.

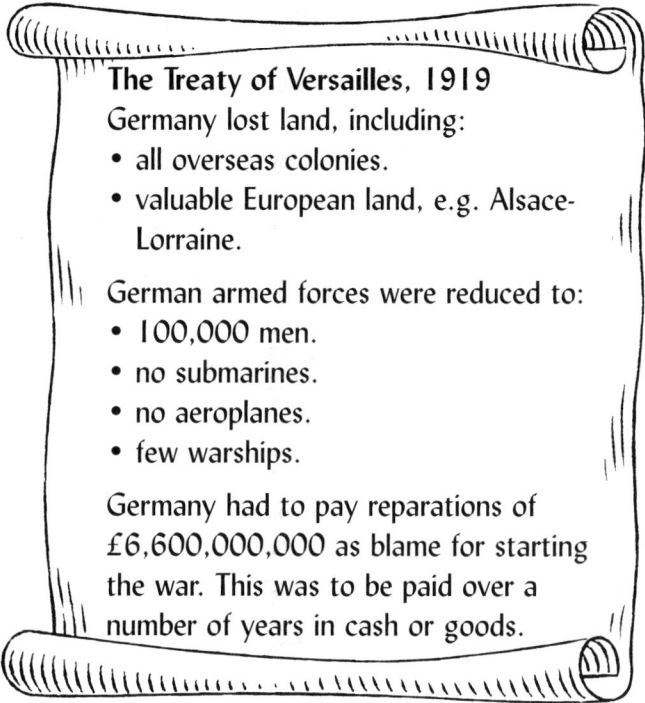

The Treaty of Versailles, 1919
Germany lost land, including:
• all overseas colonies.
• valuable European land, e.g. Alsace-Lorraine.

German armed forces were reduced to:
• 100,000 men.
• no submarines.
• no aeroplanes.
• few warships.

Germany had to pay reparations of £6,600,000,000 as blame for starting the war. This was to be paid over a number of years in cash or goods.

Unemployment in Germany 1928–1932

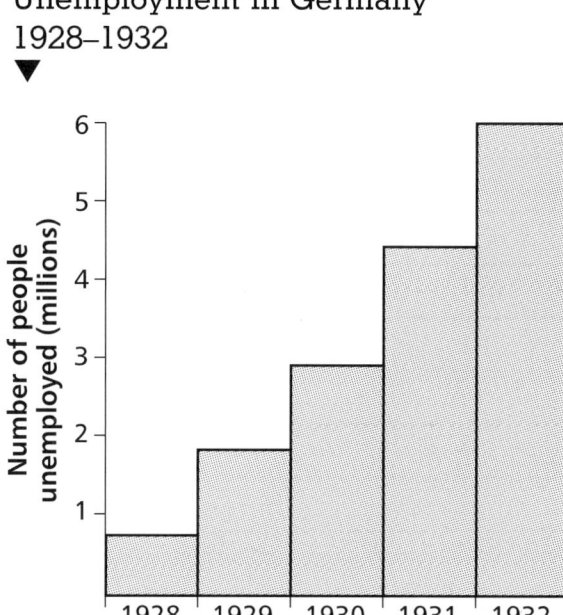

2 Use the information to complete the sections below and on the next sheet by:

a writing details of the things Hitler did that helped to make him ruler of Germany.

b writing details of other events, not caused by Hitler, that helped to make him ruler of Germany.

What Hitler did _____

_____

_____

_____

_____

_____

_____

_____

_____

C How Hitler became the German leader (continued)

Other events _____

_____

_____

_____

_____

_____

_____

_____

_____

_____

_____

_____

3 a How many different things done by Hitler have you written about?

_____

b How many different other events have you written about?

_____

c List what you think were the three most important 'things' or 'events'.

   i _____

   ii _____

   iii _____

4 Make a judgement. What was the biggest influence on Hitler becoming ruler of Germany: what he did or other events? Explain your answer.

_____

_____

_____

 C *Hitler and control of people's minds*

Look at pages 98–99 and pages 102–103 in your textbook.

You are going to write an essay to answer the question: 'How did Hitler try to control the minds of the German people?'

Read the paragraph box headings below (they are in no particular order).

Adults and propaganda • Children and anti-semitism • Children and youth movements • Hitler's reasons for trying to control minds • Whether Hitler succeeded or not in controlling minds

1 Decide which of the above headings is the Introduction and which is the Conclusion.

2 Work out an appropriate order for the other headings (e.g. chronological).

3 Write the headings in the spaces at the top of each box.

4 Write your essay by putting important relevant information into the appropriate boxes.

Introduction

You will need

C Hitler and control of people's minds (continued)

Conclusion

You will need

A Lands taken by Germany

Look at pages 51, 107 and 108 in your textbook.

Look again the map on page 51 in your textbook. This shows you the land that Germany lost at the end of the First World War. Now look at the top of pages 107 and 108, which show you the lands that Germany took between 1938 and 1939. Use this information to complete the map below.

1 Write in the four missing words.

2 Using one colour, shade in these four areas.

3 Draw an arrow from the swastika to each of the four areas.

4 List the four areas and the date each was taken in the table below.

Area	Date

B Could Hitler have been stopped?

Look at pages 107 and 108 in your textbook.

1 Read the information below.

Ⓐ By 1933 Hitler had listed the lands he wanted Germany to take. The main ones were:
- the Rhineland area of Germany (by re-militarisation).
- Austria.
- Alsace-Lorraine from France.
- the Sudetenland from Czechoslovakia.
- the Polish Corridor from Poland.
- the Ukraine from the USSR.

Ⓑ By the summer of 1938 Germany had taken:
- the Rhineland – re-militarised in 1936.
- Austria in 1938.

Ⓒ **German armed forces**

	1933	1939
Army	7 divisions	52 divisions
Navy	0 battleships	4 battleships
	0 submarines	54 submarines
Air force	0 aeroplanes	4,200 aeroplanes

Ⓓ Alliances involving Germany:
- Rome–Berlin Axis with Italy: 1936.
- Anti-Comitern Pact with Italy and Japan: 1937.

Ⓔ **The League of Nations**
- This organisation was set up in 1920 to prevent any more wars, and in the 1920s was generally successful.
- In 1931 the League failed to stop the Japanese conquest of Manchuria.
- In the years 1935 and 1936 the League failed to stop the Italian conquest of Abyssinia.

Ⓕ **Britain and France: the policy of appeasement**
- Britain and France expected the League of Nations to keep peace and had not modernised their armed forces.
- People in Britain and France did not want another war after their experience of the First World War.
- The governments of Britain and France had realised that the Treaty of Versailles had been too harsh on Germany.
- British/French policy to Germany was called 'appeasement'. It meant giving Hitler some of the lands he wanted in the hope that this would prevent a war.

You will need

B Could Hitler have been stopped? (continued)

2 From Boxes **A** and **B**, how many lands targeted by Hitler had actually been taken by 1938?

_____

3 From Boxes **C** and **D**, what methods do you think Hitler expected to use to take the other lands?

_____

_____

4 From Boxes **E** and **F**, what possible opposition was there to Hitler's plans?

_____

_____

5 Complete the table below.

Summer 1938 to autumn 1939	
Actions taken by Germany	**British/French responses**

6 Could Hitler have been stopped? Was Hitler stronger than the opposition or not?

_____

_____

_____

 C *Hitler's actions, 1936–1939*

Look at pages 104 and 106 to 108 in your textbook.

You are going to write an essay to answer the question: 'What actions taken by Hitler between 1936 and 1939 helped lead to the outbreak of the Second World War?'

Read the paragraph box headings below (they are in no particular order).

Poland • Difficulties in stopping Hitler • Austria
• The Rhineland • Czechoslovakia
• What made it easier for lands to be taken

1   Decide which of the above headings is the Introduction and which is the Conclusion.

2   Work out an appropriate order for the other headings (e.g. chronological).

3   Write the headings in the spaces at the top of each box.

4   Write your essay by putting important relevant information into the appropriate boxes.

Introduction

You will need

C Hitler's actions, 1936–1939 (continued)

Conclusion

You will need

A What was it like to be evacuated?

Look at page 109 in your textbook.

1 Look up the word 'evacuation' in a dictionary.
   What does it mean?

   _____

2 What sort of people were evacuated?

   _____

3 What kinds of places were people evacuated from?

   _____

4 What kinds of places were people evacuated to?

   _____

5 Why were people evacuated to these kinds of places?

   _____

6 Study Source **A** below. Look at two of the items each child is
   carrying. Write a sentence to say what each item was for.
   a They needed a gas mask because _____

   _____

   b They needed a label to _____

   _____

Source A Tyneside ▶
   children being
   evacuated

You will need
Dictionary

What was it like to be evacuated? (continued)

7 a Look at the sources below, which are about children's experiences of evacuation.

Source B
▼

Dear Mum,
I hope you are well. I want to come home now. Please come and get me.

Source C
▼

There was no fish shop or Woolworths or cinemas. There were no crowds of people. I felt lost.

Source D Exploring in the countryside
▼

Source E
▼

Everything was so clean. We were given face flannels and toothbrushes. We'd never cleaned our teeth until then. And hot water came from the tap. There was an indoor toilet and rooms had carpets.

Source F
▼

I was very spoilt. When my mother came to visit I prayed, 'Please God, I don't like this woman. She says she is my mother. I want to stay with my aunties.'

b Use Sources **B** to **F** to complete the table below.

The things children would have liked about evacuation	The things children would not have liked about evacuation

8 Imagine that you had been at school in the Second World War and had been evacuated.
   a Do you think you would have liked or disliked evacuation?

_____

   b Write a sentence to explain your answer to Question 8a.

_____

_____

You will need

A *The German conquest of Western Europe*

Look at the top of pages 110 to 113 in your textbook.

1   Complete the table below.

Countries that were invaded	Countries that attacked	Date

2   Choose two different colours. Colour in the countries that were invaded by land in one colour. Colour in the country that was invaded by sea in the other colour.

3   Which country did not oppose the invading German forces?

_____

4   Write down the countries that the British forces tried to defend.

_____

_____

5   Where in France did the British forces have to be evacuated from in May and June 1940?

_____

6   This evacuation took place in a hurry. What kinds of things did British forces have to leave behind or destroy?

_____

_____

_____

B The fall of France

Look at pages 112 and 113 in your textbook.

1   Read the sources below.

Source A By a French General
▼

> The German tactics of tank advances in narrow columns – assisted by fearsome dive-bombers – proved too much. They had greater fire-power and speed than our forces.

Source B By a French military planner
▼

> Not attacking through the Maginot Line ruined our defence plan. None of us military planners believed it possible to advance through the hilly forests of the Ardennes by tanks. We placed only reserve troops there. It was a clever choice of route. Their breakthrough at Sedan split our forces from British troops. After that, defeat was inevitable.

Source C By a German commander
▼

> We knew that British and French armies were advancing into Belgium to help stem our rapid attacks. Knowing we would break through at Sedan, we deliberately let them advance (we never bombed them) so they would end up being trapped. The plan worked.

Source D By a French politician
▼

> There was little enthusiasm in France for another war. Morale in the army was low – it had obsolete equipment, and generals who had very negative/defensive attitudes. French soldiers were in awe of Germany's efficient fighting forces after they had demolished Poland.

Source E By a French patriot
▼

> France might have survived the early German attacks had they not had to fight the Germans on their own. The BEF commander disobeyed orders from the French army, and chose to save his men rather than help save France.

B | *The fall of France (continued)*

2   Imagine you are General de Gaulle who had just escaped to Britain to organise a Free French Army to resist German occupation of his country. You have been instructed by the British Prime Minister, Winston Churchill, to write a secret report giving reasons why France fell. Use your textbook and the sources on the previous sheet to help you.

Report on the fall of France

TOP SECRET

1 Reasons due to good German planning/fighting

_____

_____

_____

_____

_____

2 Reasons due to poor French planning/fighting

_____

_____

_____

_____

_____

3 Reasons due to British actions

_____

_____

_____

_____

_____

_____

Signed: *General Charles de Gaulle*

You will need

C Blitzkrieg

Look at pages 110 and 112–113 in your textbook.

1   Read the notes below to help you to plan a Blitzkrieg attack.

Guidance notes
- Your aim is to conquer the area on the map below.
- You have one dive-bomber squadron, one paratroop unit, three tank units and three motorised infantry units.
- Work out your targets and which of your forces should be used on them.
- Draw arrows on the map to show your plan of attack.
- Include numbers on the arrows to show the sequence of the attack and symbols to represent air, tank or infantry.
- Remember: Air attacks preceded the ground advance, which was in narrow columns.

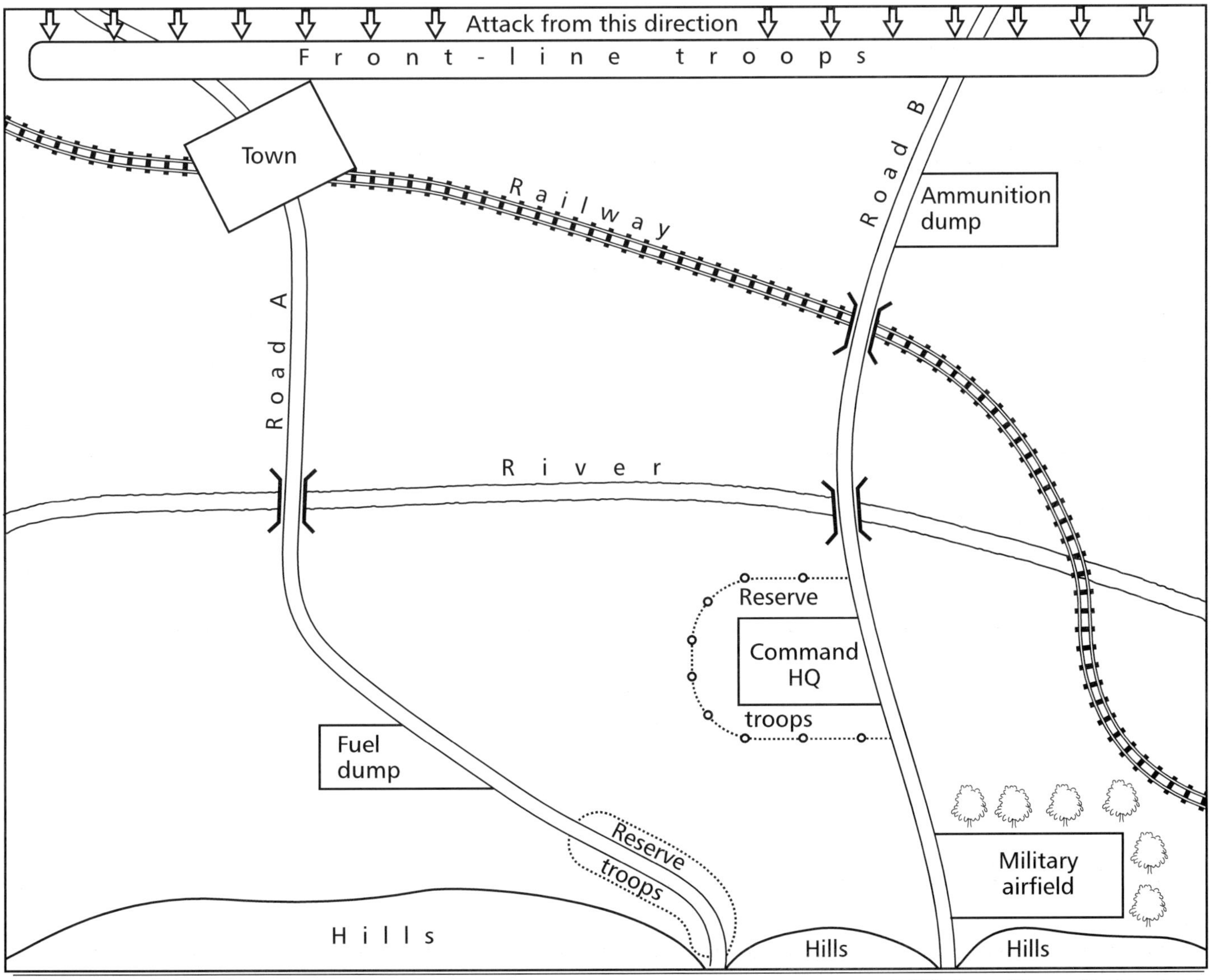

Attack from this direction

F r o n t - l i n e   t r o o p s

Town

R a i l w a y

Road A

Road B

Ammunition dump

R i v e r

Reserve

Command HQ

troops

Fuel dump

Reserve troops

Military airfield

H i l l s

Hills

Hills

C Blitzkrieg (continued)

2 Look again at the targets you decided to bomb and at those where paratroops were needed.

   a Why were some targets more suitable for bombing?

   _____

   b Why were some targets better attacked by paratroopers?

   _____

   _____

   c Which targets, if destroyed, would disrupt enemy communications?

   _____

   _____

   d Why do you think disrupting enemy communications was an important aspect of a Blitzkrieg attack?

   _____

   _____

3 Look again at your ground attacks.

   a Which did you use first: tanks or motorised infantry? Explain your choice.

   _____

   _____

   b Not all ground attack columns would be able to advance at the same speed. Explain why.

   _____

   _____

4 Think about all the different aspects of a Blitzkrieg attack. Which aspects do you think were the key to success? Explain your answer.

   _____

   _____

   _____

You will need

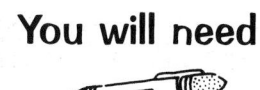

A What was it like when the bombs dropped?

Look at page 117 in your textbook.

1 Study the sources below.

Source A From a survivor of the Blitz

The siren wailed for two minutes. Then came the bombers, sounding like a deep voice saying 'where are you'. Small firebombs clattered on roofs and big bombs sounding like tearing sheets dropped from the sky. There were huge crashes as houses blew up, and then came the crackle of flames – a sort of hungry licking sound. It was frightening.

Source B From the recollections of a city girl in London in 1940

When the siren went we had to troop out of the classroom and into the air raid shelter. We sat on hard wooden benches in the dark. The noise of the bombs was terrific… we didn't listen to the teacher. It was great.

Source C This photograph shows the bombing of Coventry in 1940

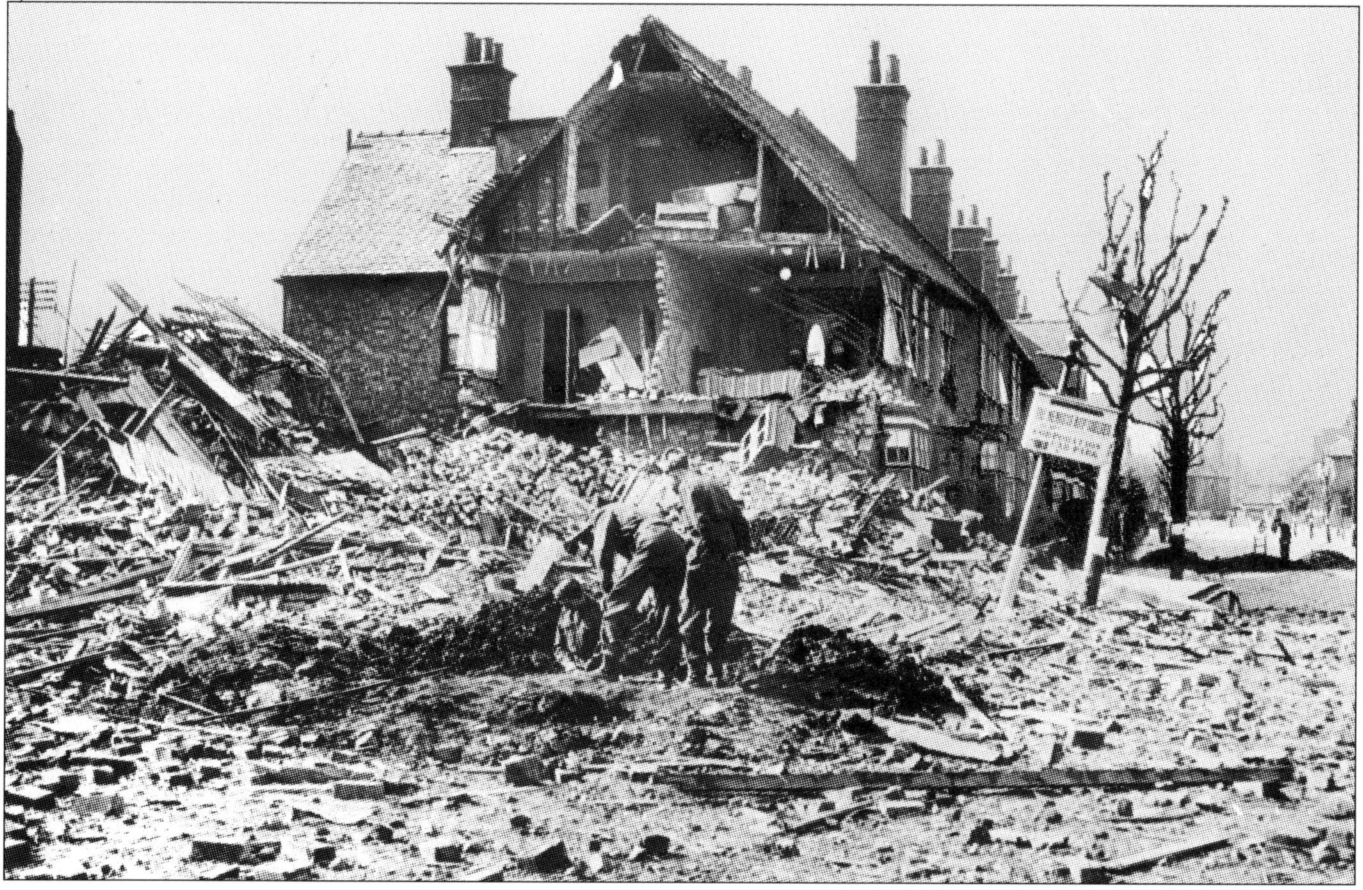

Source D Adapted from a government wartime report

A middle-aged woman who had just lost her closest relatives and her home in an air raid was advised to go and live in the country. Her attitude was that she would not let Hitler drive her out of London where she belonged.

You will need

A *What was it like when the bombs dropped? (continued)*

2 From Source **A**, write down details of any two sounds heard in an air raid.

_____

3 From Source **A**, what effect did the air raid have on the survivor?

_____

4 From Source **B**, what did the city girl think of air raids?

_____

_____

5 From Source **B**, give a reason to explain your answer to Question 4.

_____

6 From Source **C**, how much damage do you think has been done (e.g. one house destroyed)?

_____

7 From Source **C**, what might the people in the photograph be doing?

_____

_____

8 From Source **D**, how did the woman react to her losses?

_____

9 From Source **D** and page 117 in your textbook, was the woman's reaction similar or different to the reaction of other people who had suffered losses?

_____

10 From Source **D** and page 117, write a sentence to explain your answer to Question 9.

_____

_____

A *The Home Guard*

Look at page 119 in your textbook.

1 Cross out the wrong answers in the brackets below, leaving only the correct answers.

   a Men who joined the Home Guard
      (volunteered / were forced to join).

   b Many of the Home Guard were
      (of fighting age / too old for the armed forces).

   c There were (some / no) women in the Home Guard.

2 Write important details about the Home Guard below.

   a Home Guard equipment and uniforms at the start of the war.

   _____

   _____

   b Home Guard equipment and uniforms later in the war.

   _____

   _____

   c Training in the Home Guard.

   _____

   _____

   d Jobs done by the Home Guard.

   _____

   _____

3 a Do you think the Home Guard would have been able to stop
      a German invasion?

   _____

   b Write a sentence to explain your answer to Question 3a.

   _____

   _____

B Civil defence in Britain

Look at page 117 in your textbook.

1 Read the information below.

The Germans were expected to bomb industrial sites such as arms factories, which were in cities. It was assumed that air raids would take place at night, and that the pilots would know when they were flying over the cities by all the lights shining. What could be done to the windows of buildings to prevent the lights shining through? What could be done to lights in the streets? Here is one solution.

The German bombing was expected to cause more fires than the fire brigade could cope with. If fires started at home, the public would be expected to try to put them out. What equipment might they need? What methods could be used to put fires out?

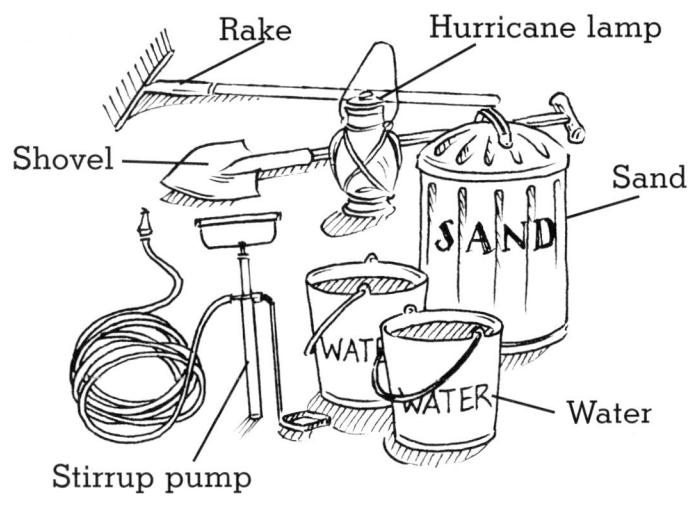

Radar would allow the RAF to have some warning of an air raid. The public also needed to know so they would have time to take cover. What could be used to warn of an air raid? What could be used to inform when the raid was over? Where could people take cover during an air raid? What was needed?

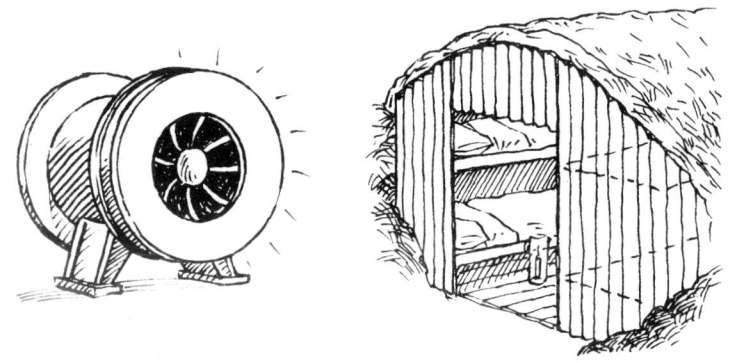

The government believed that the Germans would be able to drop bombs that released poison gas. What equipment should the public be given? How could they be warned when gas had been released? What advice should the public have about gas masks?

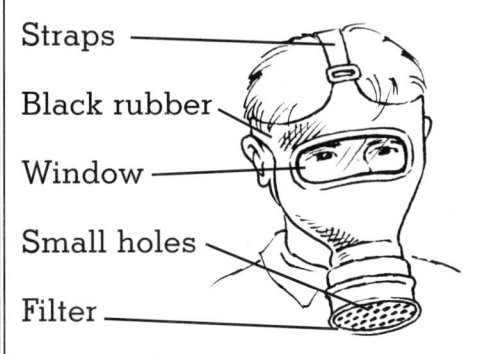

B Civil defence in Britain (continued)

2 Imagine it is September 1939 and war has just broken out. Use the information on the previous sheet to write a civil defence leaflet to explain to the public:

a the dangers posed by air raids.

b the steps taken concerning their safety.

CIVIL DEFENCE

Black out

_____

_____

_____

Fires

_____

_____

_____

Air raids

_____

_____

_____

Poison gas

_____

_____

_____

_____

B Food, fabrics and fuel

Look at page 118 in your textbook.

1 Read the information below.

Imagine it is 1943 and German U-boats have sunk a large number of ships carrying supplies to Britain. Although we produce food, fabrics and some fuel, it is not enough to cope with the demand. Will we be starved into surrender? The government is trying to cope with the shortages in three ways:
a By sharing out what is available (rationing).
b By increasing production in Britain.
c By encouraging people not to waste anything.

2 Study the sources below and on the next sheet.

Source A A ration book
▼

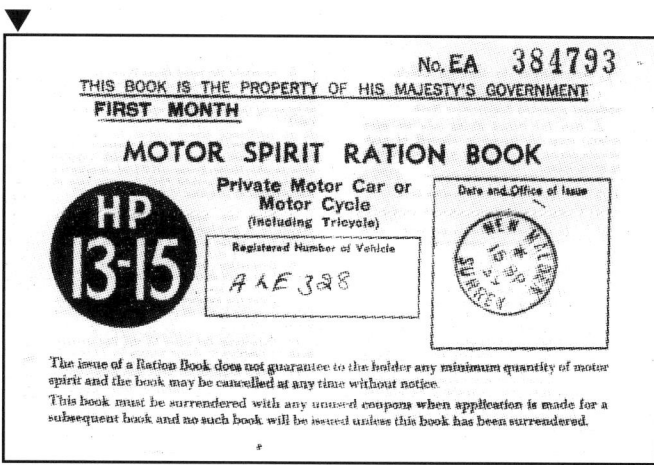

Source B A wartime recipe
▼

HOME FRONT PUDDING

Ingredients

1 cup of breadcrumbs
½ cup of dried fruit
1 cup of grated carrot
1 cup of grated potato
1 teaspoon of bicarbonate of soda
2 tablespoons of hot water

Instructions

Mix all the ingredients together.
Put the mixture in a pudding bowl.
Steam for two and a half hours.

Source C A propaganda poster
▼

Source D Food and drinks under rationing
▼

B Food, fabrics and fuel (continued)

Source E Utility clothes
▼

These are items of clothing that are useful, rather than just looking nice. They are designed to use as little material as possible, e.g. trousers without turn-ups. Designs are simple, which also means cheaper clothes.

Source F Clothing rations
▼

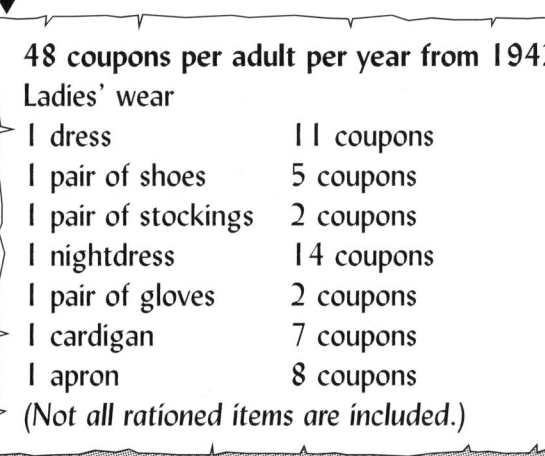

48 coupons per adult per year from 1942
Ladies' wear

1 dress	11 coupons
1 pair of shoes	5 coupons
1 pair of stockings	2 coupons
1 nightdress	14 coupons
1 pair of gloves	2 coupons
1 cardigan	7 coupons
1 apron	8 coupons

(*Not all rationed items are included.*)

Source G A wartime poster
▼

MAKE-DO AND MEND

says Mrs. Sew-and-Sew

Source H 'Bevin Boys'
▼

Every tenth conscript to the armed forces is to be sent to work in coalmines. These men are to be known as Bevin Boys after the Minister of Labour, Ernest Bevin.

Source I Tips to motorists
▼

Avoid unnecessary long journeys by car. Instead travel by bus or train.

3 Find two reasons for the shortages.

a _____ b _____

4 Write relevant information from the sources and your own ideas into the boxes on the next sheet.

B Food, fabrics and fuel (continued)

FOOD

Rationing	Increasing production	Not wasting anything

FABRICS

Rationing	Increasing production	Not wasting anything

FUEL

Rationing	Increasing production	Not wasting anything

5 From Sources **B and D**, which foods are not rationed?

_____

6 From Source **E**, do you think utility-designed clothes are popular? Explain your answer.

_____

_____

7 From Source **J**, how might you be expected to travel on short journeys?

_____

8 Do you think these measures will be enough to stop Britain being starved into surrender? Explain your answer.

_____

_____

_____

C The Battle of Britain

Look at pages 114 to 116 in your textbook.

1   Write sentences to explain what Operation Eagle and
    Operation Sea Lion were.

   a Operation Eagle was _____

   _____

   b Operation Sea Lion was _____

   _____

2   Compare the capabilities of the Luftwaffe and the RAF at the
    start of the Battle of Britain by completing the two badges
    below and on the next sheet.

The Luftwaffe

Leadership

Aeroplanes

Pilots

C / *The Battle of Britain (continued)*

The RAF

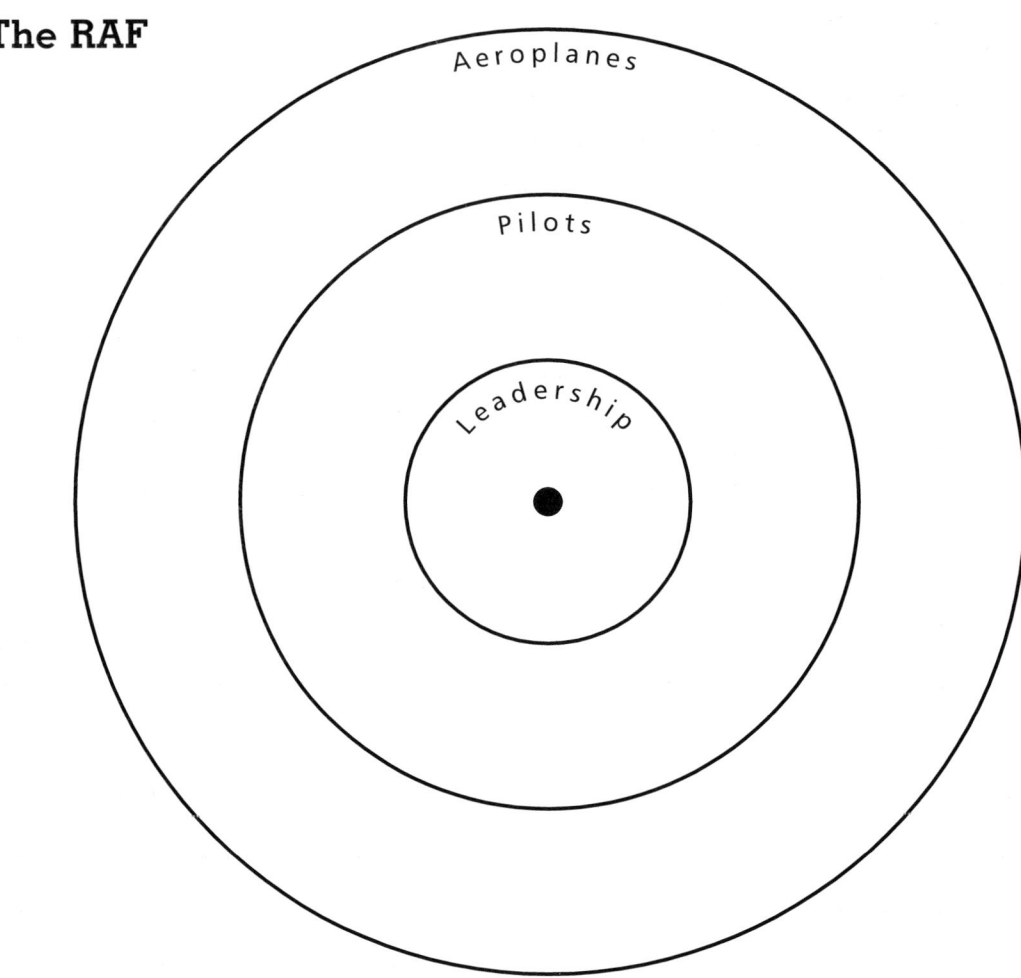

Aeroplanes

Pilots

Leadership

3 How evenly were the sides matched? Explain your answer.

_____

_____

_____

_____

4 Read the sources below and on the next sheet.

Source A From the recollections of a German
fighter pilot about the Battle of Britain

> From the very beginning the British had an
> extraordinary advantage which we could never
> overcome... the British fighter was guided all the way
> from take off to his correct position for attack on the
> German formations.

C The Battle of Britain (continued)

Source B By a recent historian

▼

Britain was slowly running out of aircraft and pilots. The German decision to switch the bombing to London relieved the pressure.

Source C Spitfire and Messerschmitt specifications

▼

Aeroplane	Top speed	Manoeuvrability	Fire power
Spitfire	600kph	Could turn very sharply	8 machine-guns
Messerschmitt ME-109	570kph	Could turn quite sharply	2 machine-guns and 2 cannons

5 Work out three reasons why the RAF won the Battle of Britain. In the boxes below, write details of the most important reason in the biggest box, details of the next most important reason in the second biggest box, and so on.

6 How important was it that the RAF won the Battle of Britain? Explain your answer.

You will need

C Feeding the family

Look at page 118 in your textbook.

1 Read the information below.

> German submarines sank so many ships carrying food supplies to
> Britain that shortages developed. This put the price of food up. The
> government set up a Ministry of Food under Lord Woolton, which began
> rationing in 1940. Gradually more and more foods were added to the
> rationed list. Attempts were made to produce more food in Britain by
> getting farmers to increase the amount of land under cultivation. Also,
> the public were encouraged to grow vegetables in their gardens.

MINISTRY  OF FOOD

Food and drinks under rationing in February 1943.
Shown as weekly allowance for one person.

Food/drink	Amount	Food/drink	Amount
Tea	2oz	Cooking fat	2oz
Cheese	3oz	Sausages	2oz
Fresh meat	To the value of 1s 2d	Coffee	2oz
Fresh eggs	1	Bacon	4oz
Margarine	4oz	Sugar	8oz
Butter	6oz	Sweets	5 points
Fresh milk	3 pints	Jam	4oz

2 Compare the rationed items for January 1940 in your textbook
with the ones above for February 1943. What differences can
you find?

_____

_____

_____

3 Choose three colours. In the table above, colour in all the
meats in one colour, the drinks in another colour and the dairy
foods in the third colour.

4 List below any foods likely to have been popular in the 1940s
that were not rationed.

_____

_____

You will need

C Feeding the family (continued)

5 Look again at your answer to Question 4. Why do you think these foods were not rationed?

_____

_____

6 Look again at the information on the previous sheet. What other places may have been converted to growing crops?

_____

_____

7 The public were also encouraged to keep animals to provide food. What kinds of animals for what kind of food?

Animal   Food

_____   _____

_____   _____

_____   _____

8 Create a menu for two adults for one week in February 1943. Remember that you cannot exceed the amounts for rationed items, but you can eat much more unrationed food. Food substitutes were available, e.g. dried eggs and powdered milk.

Day	Breakfast	Lunch	Tea
Sunday			
Monday			
Tuesday			
Wednesday			
Thursday			
Friday			
Saturday			

9 The wartime diet was nutritious but boring. What proof of this have you found?

_____

_____

_____

You will need

A Operation Barbarossa

Look at pages 122 and 123 in your textbook.

1 Complete the sentences in the boxes below.

Sleet and rain created mud, which stopped _____ _____ _____ _____	Russian partisans were ordered to sabotage _____ _____ _____ _____	Very low temperatures in December caused soldiers without winter clothing to _____ _____ _____
Very low temperatures in December stopped the advance because _____ _____ _____ _____	When the mud froze over _____ _____ _____ _____	Stalin tried to get supplies from _____ _____ _____ _____
Factories were dismantled and moved away from the fighting. There they were _____ _____ _____	Stalin ordered locomotives and food to be destroyed, so the Germans _____ _____ _____	Russian forces fought bravely and _____ _____ _____ _____

2 Decide which boxes show how Russian efforts (as opposed to the weather) helped stop the Germans. Cut out the Russian symbols below and stick one at the top of each of these boxes.

B A *soldier's view of Operation Barbarossa*

Look at pages 121 to 123 in your textbook.

Imagine you are a senior German officer involved in Operation Barbarossa. At the end of each day you write down the things that have happened, including your thoughts and feelings.

1   Look at pages 121 and 122. Write an entry in your diary for late July 1941.

JULY

Day:_____   Date: _____

German advance:

_____

_____

_____

_____

_____

_____

Russian defence:

_____

_____

_____

_____

_____

_____

My view on the likely outcome of the attack:

_____

_____

_____

_____

_____

 B A *soldier's view of Operation Barbarossa (continued)*

2   Look at page 123 in your textbook. Write an entry in your diary below for mid December 1941.

DECEMBER

Day:_____   Date: _____

German advance:

_____

_____

_____

_____

_____

_____

Bad weather:

_____

_____

_____

_____

_____

My view on the likely outcome of the attack:

_____

_____

_____

---

3   Look again at the two pages of your diary. What changes can you find?

_____

_____

_____

_____

 Pearl Harbor: conspiracy or carelessness?

Look at pages 125 and 126 in your textbook.

1 Read the sources below and on the next sheet.

Source A Countdown to the attacks
▼

	Sunday, December 7, 1941
6.10am	Japanese launch first wave of 183 aircraft from carriers situated 250km north of Pearl Harbor.
7.02am	Opana radar station on Oahu Island: Privates Elliott and Lockhard notice what appears to be a flight of unidentified aircraft heading for Oahu.
7.10am	Elliott telephones his superiors at Fort Shafter, but only Lieutenant Tyler (a trainee) is on duty because it is a Sunday morning.
7.15am	Japanese launch second wave of 168 aircraft carriers.
7.20am	Lieutenant Tyler decides that the unidentified aircraft are US airforce B-17s scheduled to land on Oahu. He orders Opana radar station to close down.
7.39am	Elliott and Lockhard disobey orders and continue to monitor unidentified aircraft. They lose aircraft from radar screen 32km from Oahu due to shadow caused by surrounding hills.
7.50am	First wave of Japanese aircraft bomb US naval base at Pearl Harbor on Oahu Island.
8.55am	Second wave of Japanese aircraft bomb Pearl Harbor.

Source B Adapted from a recent book about Pearl Harbor
▼

Roosevelt ordered the fleet to Pearl Harbor and was determined to keep it there despite warnings from the navy that there was inadequate protection from air and torpedo attacks... when told by Admiral Turner in June 1941 that shutting off American oil to Japan would very likely lead to war in the Pacific, Roosevelt immediately froze all Japanese assets in the USA. This left them unable to buy US oil.

Source C By Winston Churchill, December 1941
▼

From the end of 1940 the Americans had pierced vital Japanese ciphers and were decoding their military and diplomatic telegrams.

Source D Adapted from *The Modern World Since 1870* by L E Snellgrove (Longman, 1977)
▼

Luck was with the Japanese because for most of the voyage bad weather had cut down visibility... Japanese ships were never seen by US scouting aircraft because they were patrolling in the wrong area – south-west of Oahu.

 Pearl Harbor: conspiracy or carelessness? (continued)

Source E From the research of an American historian
▼

> Numerous warnings were sent to Roosevelt between June and December 1941 about a possible attack on Pearl Harbor.
> • July 10 – US military attaché in Tokyo reported Japan practising air attacks on ships in Ariake Bay [which closely resembled Pearl Harbor].
> • September 24 – Japanese were looking for exact locations of ships in Pearl Harbor.
> • November 29 – Japanese Embassy in USA received the message that zero hour was to be December 7.
> • None of these or numerous other messages reached commanders at Pearl Harbor.

2 If there was a conspiracy, what do you think was Roosevelt's motive?

_____

_____

3 Complete the table below by selecting evidence from Sources **A** to **E**.

Evidence of conspiracy	Evidence of carelessness

4 Look again at your answer to Question 3. Was the bombing of Pearl Harbor a conspiracy or carelessness or both? Explain your answer.

_____

_____

_____

_____

 ## *The Battle of Stalingrad*

Look at page 128 in your textbook.

1   Fill in the missing words in the paragraph below.

The Battle of Stalingrad was fought in the years _____
and _____ . The city could not be _____ , and
so had to be taken by direct _____ . All-out attack was
ordered by General _____ , commander of the
_____ _____ Army. An important part of the
battle was when the Russians just managed to hold onto a narrow
_____ . Then they counter-attacked and cut off
_____ German soldiers. The German air force
(_____) could not drop enough supplies to their army
colleagues. On February 1 the Germans surrendered, having lost
_____ men in the battle.

2   Study the sources below. These show different stages in the
Battle of Stalingrad. Next to each photograph, describe what is
happening.

Source A German soldiers

Source B Russian soldiers

_____   _____

_____   _____

_____   _____

_____   _____

A *The Battle of Stalingrad (continued)*

Source C ▶

_____

_____

_____

_____

_____

◀ Source D

_____

_____

_____

_____

_____

_____

Source E ▶

_____

_____

_____

_____

_____

B The Battle of El Alamein

Look at pages 129 and 130 in your textbook.

1 Study the sources below.

Source A From *Headline History: The 20th Century* by J Ray, (Evans Bros, 1978)

▼

The British 8th Army consisted of some 220,000 men organised into 3 army corps. They were supported by more than 1,000 guns. About 1,100 tanks were ready for the action. Overhead, planes of the RAF had almost total control. The Afrika Corps had only 105,000 men, less than half of whom were German. They had just over 300 tanks.

Source B Adapted from *The Life and Death of the Afrika Corps* by R Lewin, written in 1972

▼

Within a very short time of becoming commander of the 8th Army, General Montgomery imposed his will on his officer corps and his personality on his troops.

Source C From a school textbook on the Second World War

▼

After defeat by Rommel's Afrika Corps at Tobruk, British forces retreated a long way until they could take up excellent defensive positions at El Alamein. This site was at the end of a 40-mile [65-km] wide corridor that was flanked by the sea and the impossible tar sands of the Qattara Depression. At this point the Afrika Corps already had over-stretched supply lines and so Rommel was not guaranteed reserves of men or weapons.

Source D From *A Man Called Intrepid* by W Stevenson, 1976

▼

Ultra [the British decoding machine] picked up German signals disclosing that Rommel had quit the desert to be treated for chronic stomach ailments and poor circulation.

Ⓐ	Qattara Depression
➡①➡	Advance of Afrika Corps
➡②➡	Retreat of Afrika Corps
➡①➡	Advance of 8th Army
⋯②⋯➤	Advance of British and US troops to Afrika Corps

Source E

▼

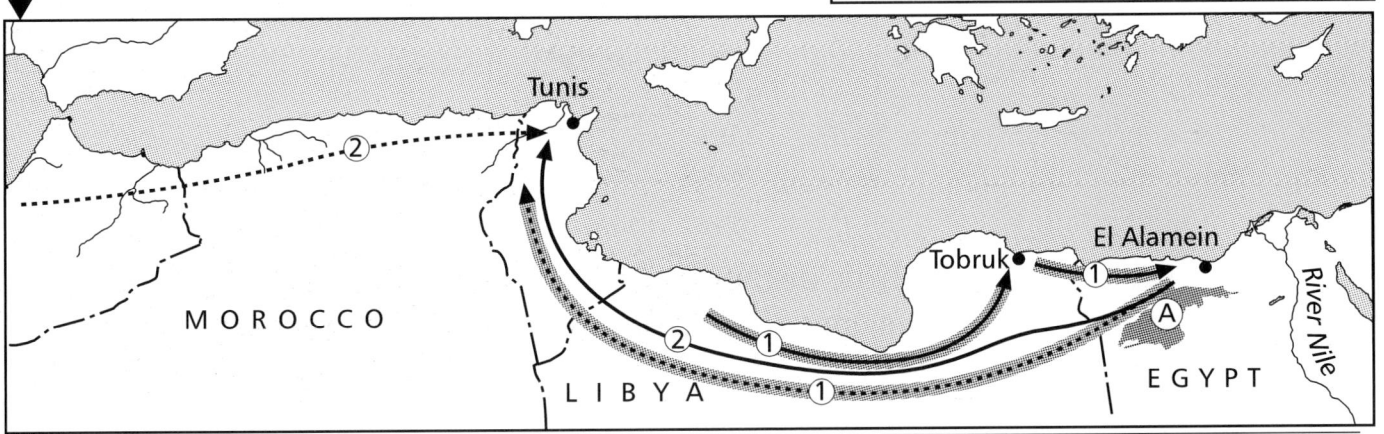

 B **The Battle of El Alamein (continued)**

2 Using the sources and your textbook, complete the diagram below by:

  a writing the reasons for the British victory at El Alamein in the circles.

  b writing the results of the British victory at El Alamein in the boxes.

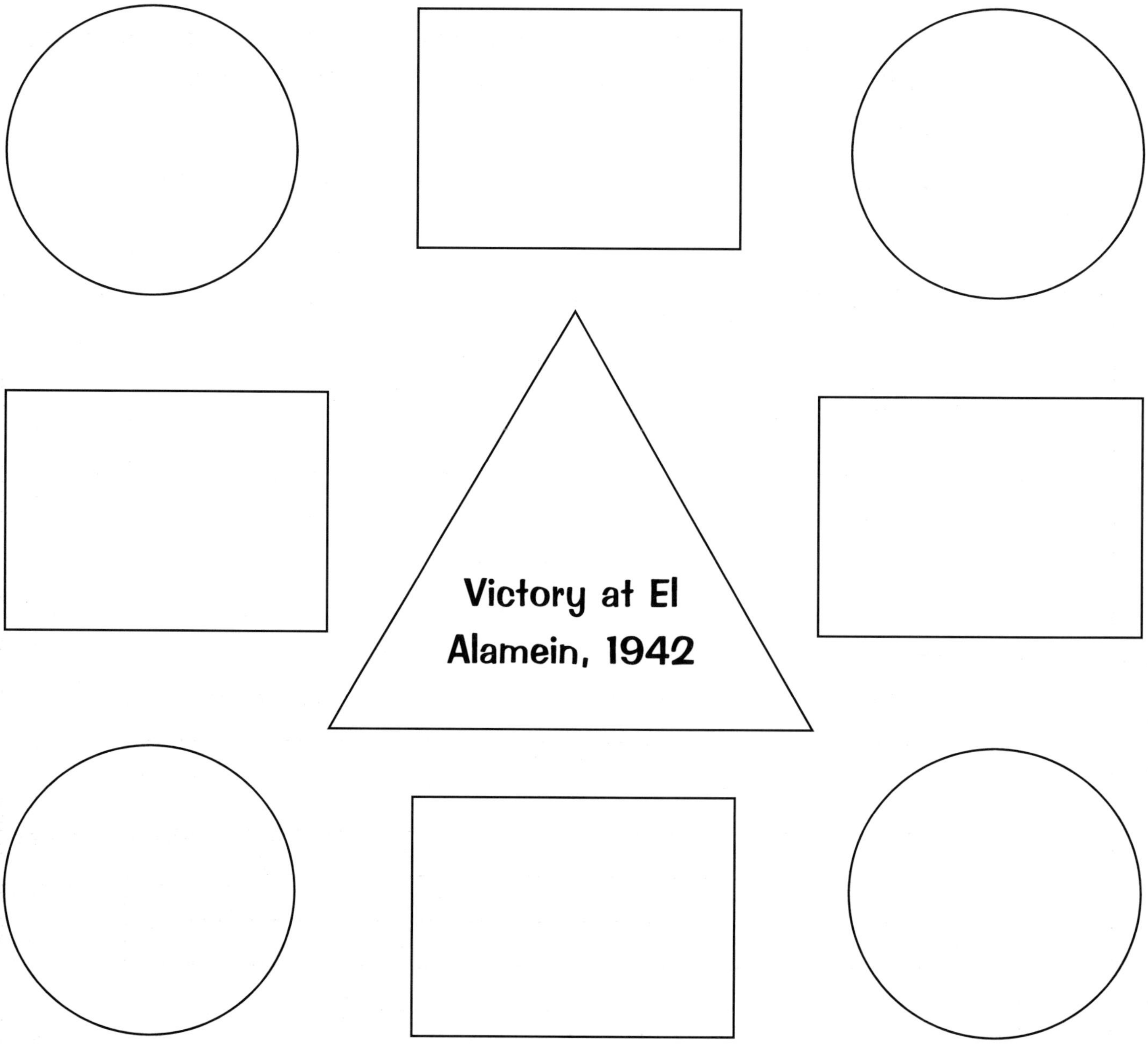

Victory at El Alamein, 1942

3 Draw arrows to link each circle and box with the triangle. Work out which arrows should point towards the triangle, and which should point away from it.

C Stalingrad and El Alamein

Look at pages 128 to 129 in your textbook.

Imagine you have been asked to fill two display cabinets in a new Second World War museum with writing and memorabilia.

1 Write an account of the Battle of Stalingrad in the cabinet below, and of El Alamein on the next sheet. Use some of these headings to help you:

The two sides • Location of the battle • Scale • Weapons used • Conditions/weather • An important incident/decision • Importance of the battle.

CABINET A

The Battle of _____ Date _____

You will need

C Stalingrad and El Alamein (continued)

CABINET B

The Battle of ____________________ Date ___________

____

____

____

2 Write down what memorabilia you could put inside each cabinet.

Cabinet A ____________________________________

____

Cabinet B ____________________________________

____

3 What original documents might it be worth displaying?

____

You will need

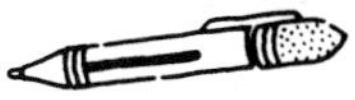

A Equipment and devices

Look at page 133 in your textbook.

1 Study the illustrations below.

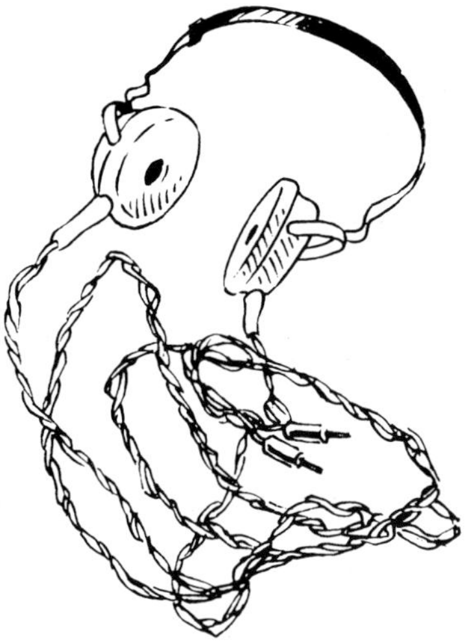

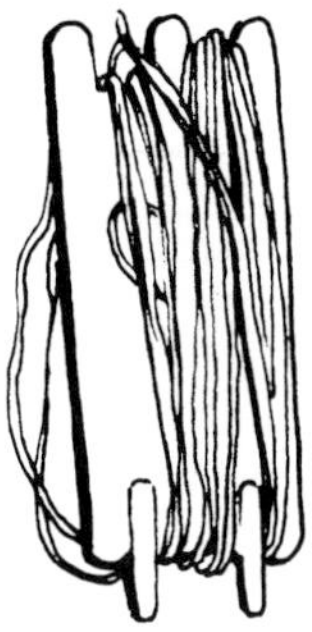

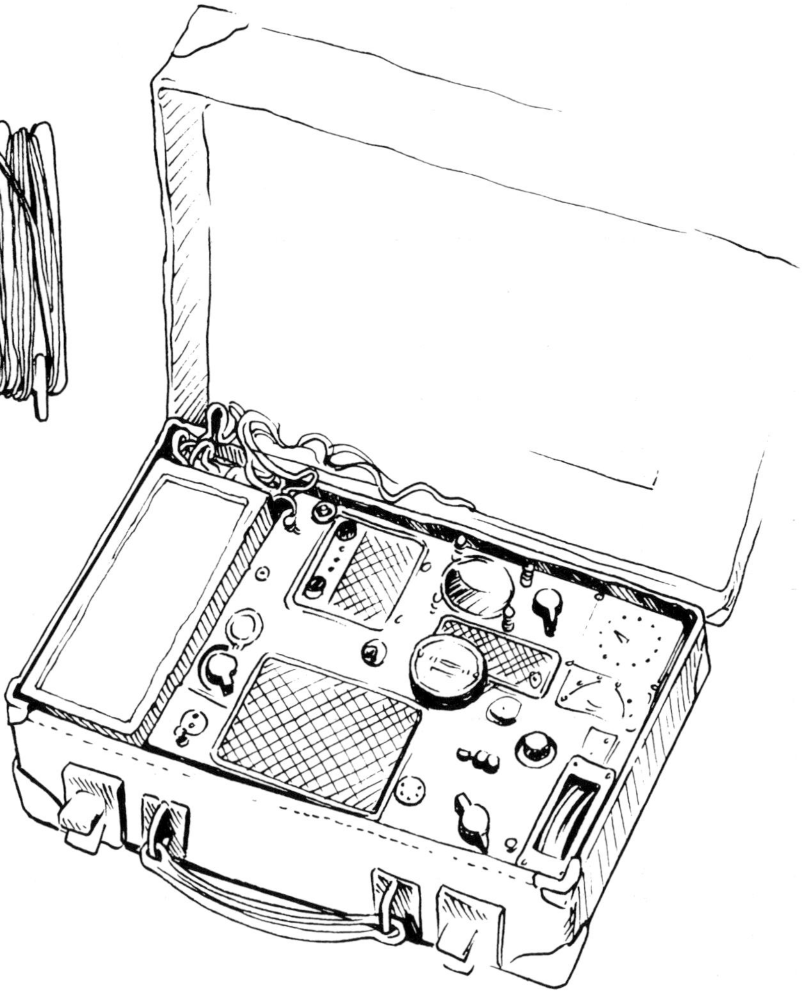

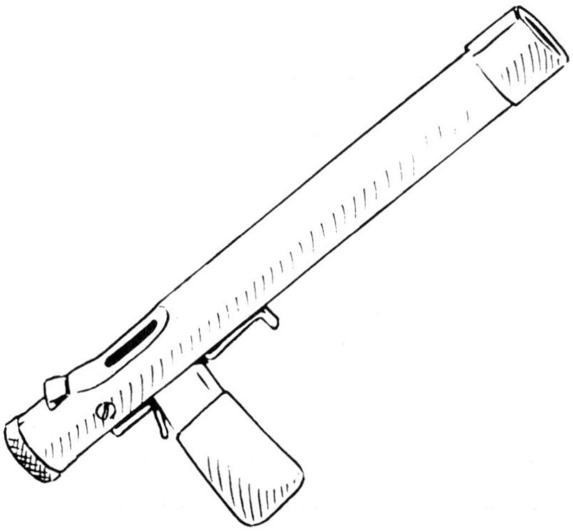

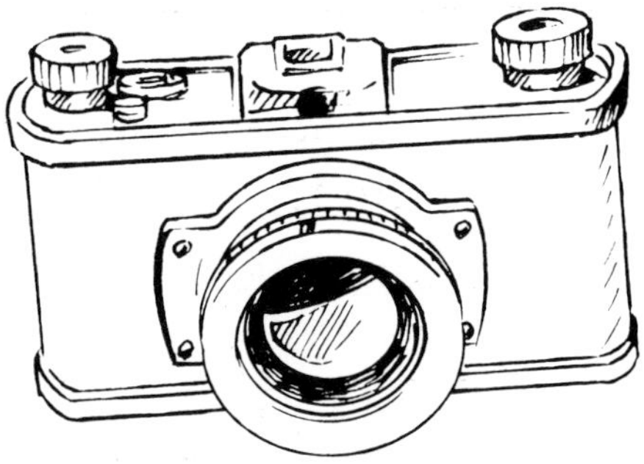

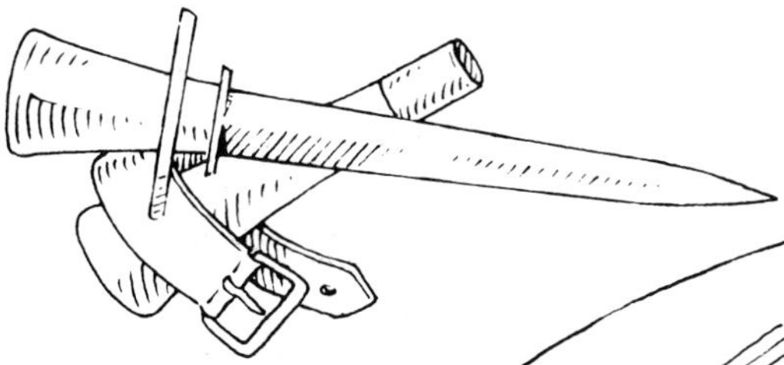

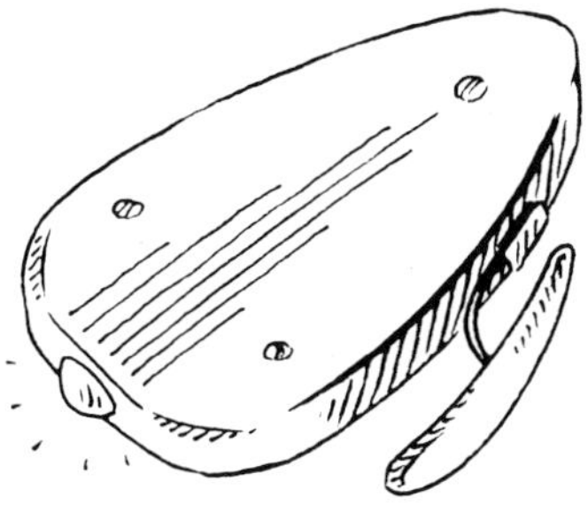

You will need

A Equipment and devices (continued)

2 Using the illustrations on the previous sheet, complete the table below.

Name of equipment	What it might be used for

3 Look at page 133 in your textbook. Write down any other equipment that caused explosions.

_____

_____

_____

4 Write a couple of sentences about a successful SOE operation.

_____

_____

_____

_____

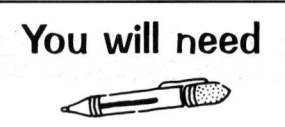

You will need

B Allied prisoners of war

1 Read the information below.

Thousands of Allied servicemen, particularly air crews shot down on bombing raids, were rounded up by the Germans and placed in prisoner-of-war camps. Once there, it was the duty of every serviceman to try to escape and somehow get back to Britain so he could fight again.

2 Look at the plan of a prisoner-of-war camp below.

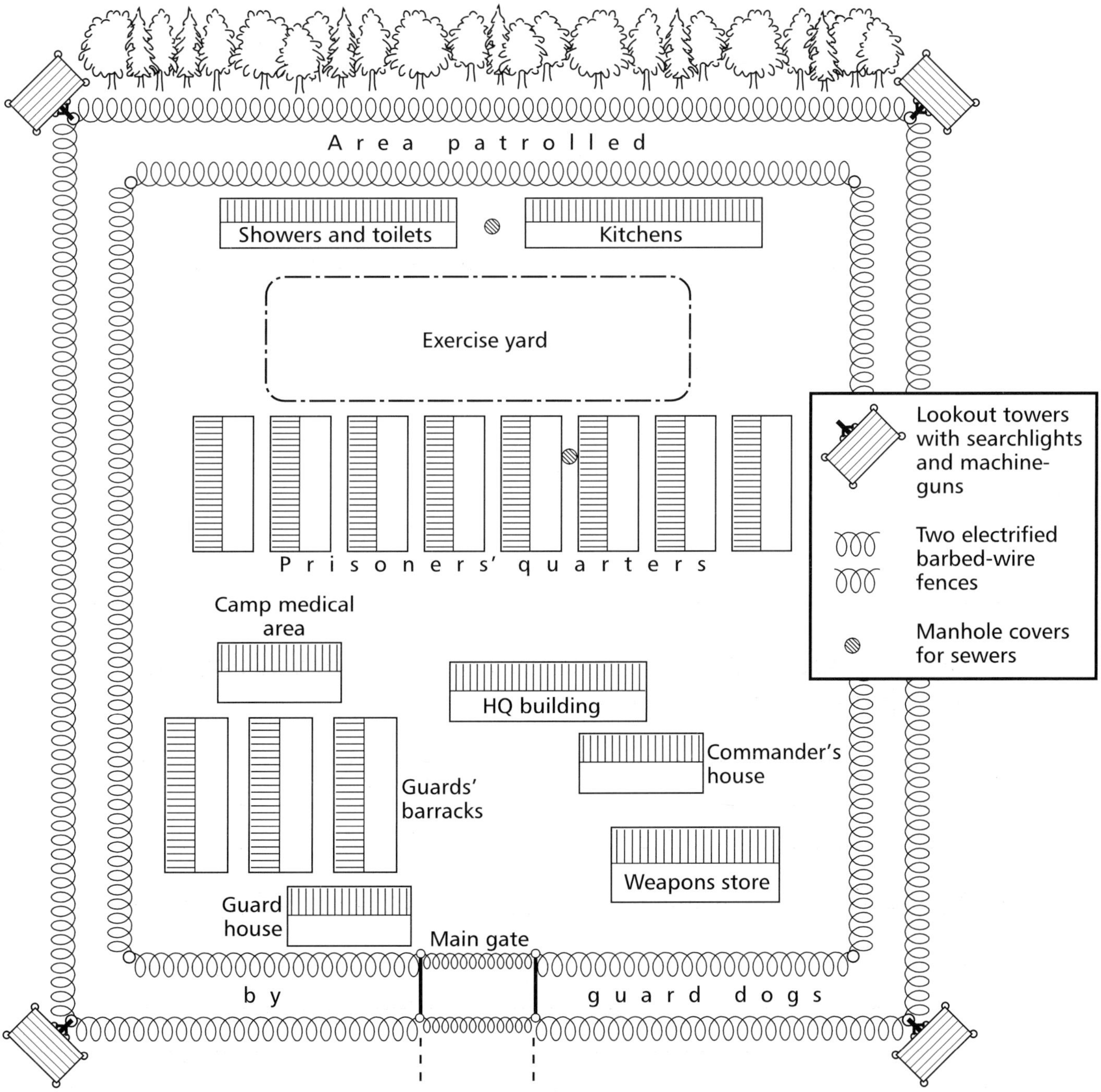
Area patrolled
Showers and toilets
Kitchens
Exercise yard
Prisoners' quarters
Camp medical area
HQ building
Commander's house
Guards' barracks
Weapons store
Guard house
Main gate
by guard dogs
Lookout towers with searchlights and machine-guns
Two electrified barbed-wire fences
Manhole covers for sewers

You will need

B Allied prisoners of war (continued)

3 Using the plan of the prison camp, explain how you would try to escape.

_____

_____

_____

_____

_____

_____

_____

_____

4 a In the table below, make a list of the things you would need once you were outside the camp.

   b Say briefly what you would need these things for.

Things needed	Why necessary?

5 What things might go wrong in your escape attempt?

_____

_____

_____

_____

_____

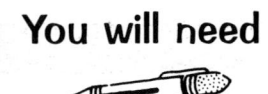

 Recruiting and training secret agents

Look at pages 132 to 134 in your textbook.

1   Read the information below.

> **Some of the jobs done by Resistance groups in occupied Europe**
> * Establish or maintain Resistance groups.
> * Print/distribute anti-Nazi propaganda.
> * Assassinate important Nazis.
> * Carry out acts of sabotage, e.g. blow up arms dumps.

2   What other jobs do you think Resistance groups did?

   _____

   _____

   _____

   _____

3   Imagine you are a senior officer in the SOE who has the task of overseeing the recruitment and training of secret agents to be sent to France in the Second World War. Agents were often recruited on recommendation by other SOE members or were drawn from the armed services. Sometimes adverts were placed in British newspapers seeking French people to become agents.

   a Devise such an advert, bearing in mind the need for security.

   ┌───┐
   │   **Job vacancies**   │
   │ _____   │
   │ _____   │
   │ _____   │
   │ _____   │
   │ _____   │
   │ _____   │
   │ _____   │
   └───┘

C *Recruiting and training secret agents (continued)*

Normally successful candidates underwent two separate interviews, with an M15 security screening in between.

b As the interviewer, what sort of things would you want to know about the candidate's professional capabilities?

_____

_____

_____

_____

_____

_____

_____

c What sort of things would you want to know about the candidate's personal qualities?

_____

_____

_____

_____

_____

_____

d Would you tell them just how serious the risk to their lives would be if they were sent to France? Explain your answer.

_____

_____

_____

_____

_____

_____

_____

 C *Recruiting and training secret agents (continued)*

Once accepted, candidates had to undergo about 8 weeks of training (22 weeks for radio operators) in different locations throughout Britain. Two aspects involved physical fitness and handling small guns.

e Work out a training programme by listing any aspect that you think would have been important (you should include the two examples given above). Next to each aspect, explain why you have included it in the training programme.

_____

_____

_____

_____

_____

_____

_____

_____

_____

_____

f Bearing in mind your previous answers, what weapons and equipment do you think new secret agents should have been parachuted into France with?

_____

_____

_____

_____

_____

_____

_____

_____

_____

_____

ABC *The secret agent's game*

Note to teacher

Please enlarge the board game on page 161 to A3 size.

Introduction

You are a newly trained SOE secret agent, who, together with three other agents, is to be parachuted into France. Your mission is to blow up an arms factory before the new weapon being made there is moved out for use against Britain. You are working against the clock.

How to play

1 Before you start:

   a Get into groups of four people, each one a secret agent.

   b Each player should have one counter.

   c Only one dice is needed per group.

2 Playing the game:

   a Each player throws the dice – whoever rolls the highest number goes first.

   b Each player throws the dice in turn.

   c If your counter lands on an information square, simply follow the instructions. If the news is good, you may be able to have another turn or move your counter forwards. If the news is bad, you may have to miss a turn or move your counter backwards. If the news if really bad, you may be out of the game.

   d You can judge whether you have reached the arms factory in time by keeping count of the number of throws of the dice: nine or fewer throws means that you have blown up the factory before the new weapon is moved out.

ABC The secret agent's game (continued)

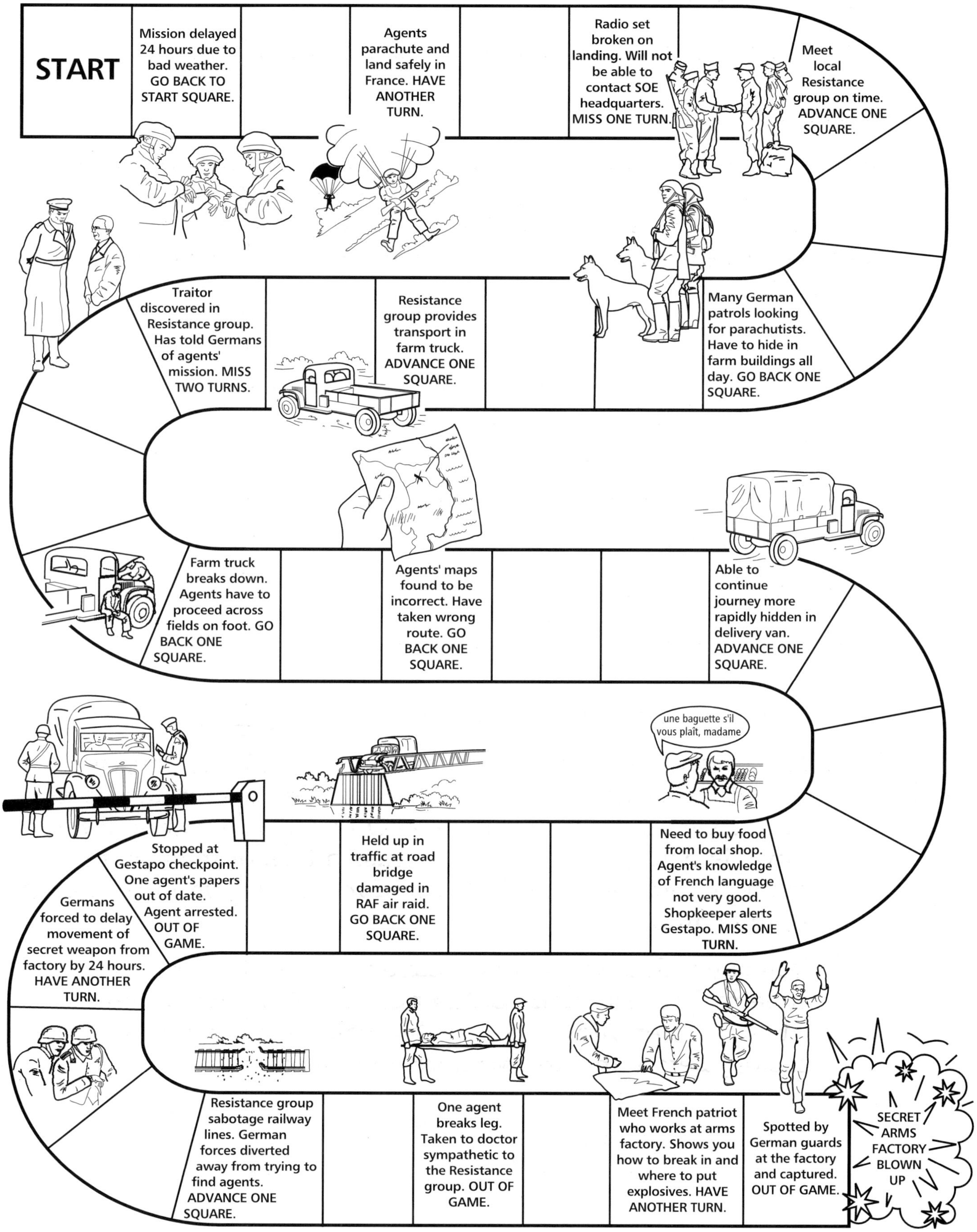

START

Mission delayed 24 hours due to bad weather. GO BACK TO START SQUARE.

Agents parachute and land safely in France. HAVE ANOTHER TURN.

Radio set broken on landing. Will not be able to contact SOE headquarters. MISS ONE TURN.

Meet local Resistance group on time. ADVANCE ONE SQUARE.

Many German patrols looking for parachutists. Have to hide in farm buildings all day. GO BACK ONE SQUARE.

Traitor discovered in Resistance group. Has told Germans of agents' mission. MISS TWO TURNS.

Resistance group provides transport in farm truck. ADVANCE ONE SQUARE.

Farm truck breaks down. Agents have to proceed across fields on foot. GO BACK ONE SQUARE.

Agents' maps found to be incorrect. Have taken wrong route. GO BACK ONE SQUARE.

Able to continue journey more rapidly hidden in delivery van. ADVANCE ONE SQUARE.

une baguette s'il vous plaît, madame

Stopped at Gestapo checkpoint. One agent's papers out of date. Agent arrested. OUT OF GAME.

Held up in traffic at road bridge damaged in RAF air raid. GO BACK ONE SQUARE.

Need to buy food from local shop. Agent's knowledge of French language not very good. Shopkeeper alerts Gestapo. MISS ONE TURN.

Germans forced to delay movement of secret weapon from factory by 24 hours. HAVE ANOTHER TURN.

Resistance group sabotage railway lines. German forces diverted away from trying to find agents. ADVANCE ONE SQUARE.

One agent breaks leg. Taken to doctor sympathetic to the Resistance group. OUT OF GAME.

Meet French patriot who works at arms factory. Shows you how to break in and where to put explosives. HAVE ANOTHER TURN.

Spotted by German guards at the factory and captured. OUT OF GAME.

SECRET ARMS FACTORY BLOWN UP

A | *The Battle of the Atlantic*

Look at pages 135 and 136 in your textbook.

1   Read the labels below.

(ASDIC) (Convoys) (Radar) (Mines) (Torpedoes) (Depth charges)

2   Write the correct labels next to the matching pictures below
     and on the next sheet.

3   Write one or two sentences to explain what each picture
     shows.

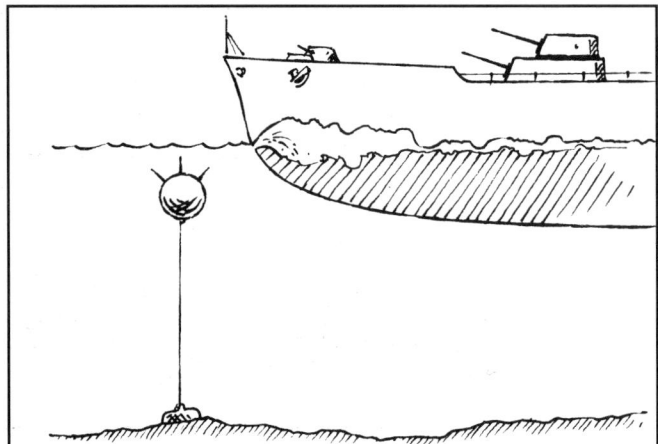

◀ Label _____

Sentences _____

_____

_____

_____

_____

Label _____

Sentences _____

_____

_____

_____

_____

 ▶

◀ Label _____

Sentences _____

_____

_____

_____

_____

A The Battle of the Atlantic (continued)

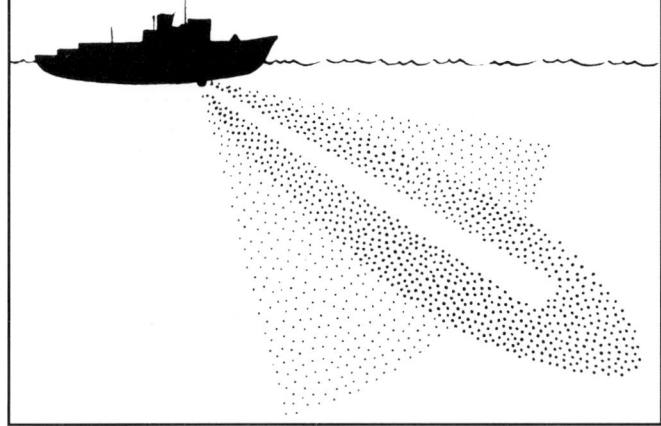

◄ Label _____

Sentences _____

_____

_____

_____

Label _____

Sentences _____

_____

_____

_____

 ▶

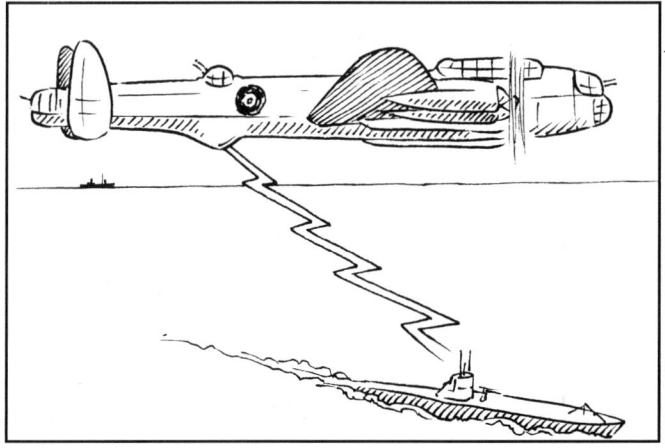

◄ Label _____

Sentences _____

_____

_____

_____

4 Look again at your answers to Questions 2 and 3.

    a Choose the labels that are about **finding** German submarines. Write these below.

_____

    b Choose the labels that are about **destroying** German submarines. Write these below.

_____

You will need

B Sink the Bismarck

Look at page 135 in your textbook.

1 Read the information below.

> **Background**
> The world's most powerful battleship, the *Bismarck*, left Gdynia in German-occupied Poland with the cruiser *Prince Eugen* and sailed via Bergen and north of Iceland to the Denmark Straits (between Greenland and Iceland). The mission was to attack Allied convoys crossing the Atlantic Ocean bringing in vital supplies to Britain.

Date	Time	The timetable of events
May 24, 1941	5.30am 5.52am 6.00am	Two German ships spotted by HMS *Hood* and *Prince of Wales*. Enemy ships shell each other. HMS *Hood* sunk. Of 1,429 crew, only 3 survive. HMS *Prince of Wales* escapes. HMS *Hood*: 8 x 15-inch guns, 12 x 6-inch guns, 32 knots top speed
	4.00pm	Message from Admiralty: all available Royal Navy vessels to find and sink the *Bismarck*.
	11.55pm	Bomber aircraft from the carrier *Victorious* cause slight damage to *Bismarck*.
May 25, 1941		Contact with *Bismarck* lost. Admiralty believe she will steer a course for the French port of Brest for repairs.
May 26, 1941	9.00am	*Bismarck* sighted 1,600km from Brest, but too far for Royal Navy ships to catch up.
	10.00pm	Bombers from carrier *Ark Royal* attack *Bismarck* and damage her rudder. She cannot steer and is sailing around in circles, allowing Royal Navy vessels to catch up.
May 27, 1941	8.47am 10.00am 10.40am	Royal Navy battleships *King George V* and *Rodney* shell *Bismarck*, putting her guns out of action. *Bismarck* reduced to a blazing wreck, but still afloat. *Bismarck* sunk by torpedo from the cruiser *Dorsetshire*. Of 2,500 crew, only 117 survive. The *Bismarck*: 8 x 15-inch guns, 12 x 6-inch guns, 29 knots top speed

You will need

B Sink the Bismarck (continued)

2 On the map below:

a complete the missing words.

b draw on the route of the *Bismarck* with arrows and write on relevant dates.

c write in briefly what happened at each ⊗.

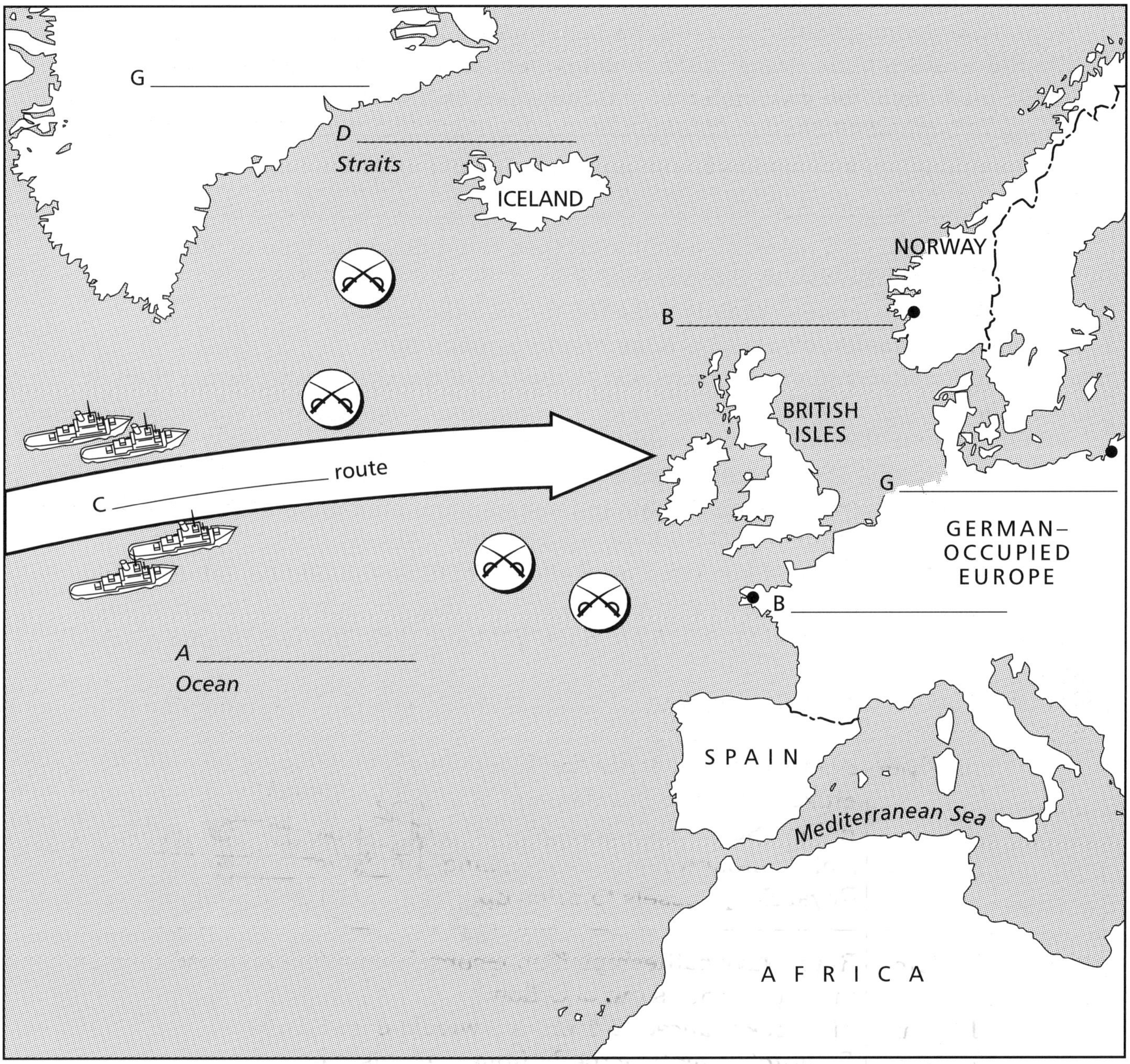

G _____

D _____
Straits

ICELAND

NORWAY

B _____

BRITISH
ISLES

route

C _____

G _____

GERMAN-
OCCUPIED
EUROPE

A _____
Ocean

B _____

SPAIN

Mediterranean Sea

AFRICA

3 Look again at the timetable of events on the previous sheet. Choose two different colours. Colour around the areas that show British successes in one colour and the areas that show German successes in the other colour.

C The Dambusters' raid

Look at page 137 in your textbook.

1 Study the information below and on the next sheet.

The idea
The Moehne, Eder, Sorpe and other dams were believed to control the water needed to provide hydro-electric power to the factories in Germany's industrial heartland, the Rühr valley. If the dams could be breached, serious and long-term damage could be done to the production of war materials and weapons.

A lot of thought and research was undertaken to produce the type of weapon that could successfully breach these dams.

- The dam area was too heavily guarded to use saboteurs.
- Torpedoes would not work because of anti-torpedo nets.
- Conventional bombs would explode at the top of the dam walls, rather than at the base.
- The inventor, Barnes Wallis, developed a bouncing bomb, cylindrical in shape and weighing 4,196kg. If dropped at 18 metres above the surface and 400 metres from the dam walls, it would rotate in backspin and sink to near the base. The explosion would cause shock waves, making the walls crumble.
- Four-engined Lancaster bombers were chosen to drop the bombs, but these needed two spotlights to be installed to ensure that air crews knew when they were exactly 18 metres above the surface (at that height the two beams crossed).

 # The Dambusters' raid (continued)

The training

The raid required great skill and experience, and so, in March 1943, a special squadron (617) was created. It was led by Wing Commander Guy Gibson, who personally hand-picked his crews. They underwent rigorous training in the Lake and Peak Districts of England, where the terrain was similar to the dam area in Germany.

The raid took place on the night of the May 17, 1943 using 19 Lancasters. To avoid detection, the planes flew at very low altitude and crews observed strict radio silence.

Nine Lancasters headed for the Moehne Dam. In the first attack, Gibson's bomb exploded short of the dam wall. Heavy anti-aircraft fire from the ground prevented the next three attacks from succeeding. In the fifth attack, two Lancasters flanked the one trying to drop the bomb to shield it from anti-aircraft fire.

The flanking worked and Flight Lieutenant Maltby's bomb successfully breached the dam. Meanwhile, Pilot Officer Knight's bomb destroyed the Eder Dam. All attempts to destroy the Sorpe Dam failed.

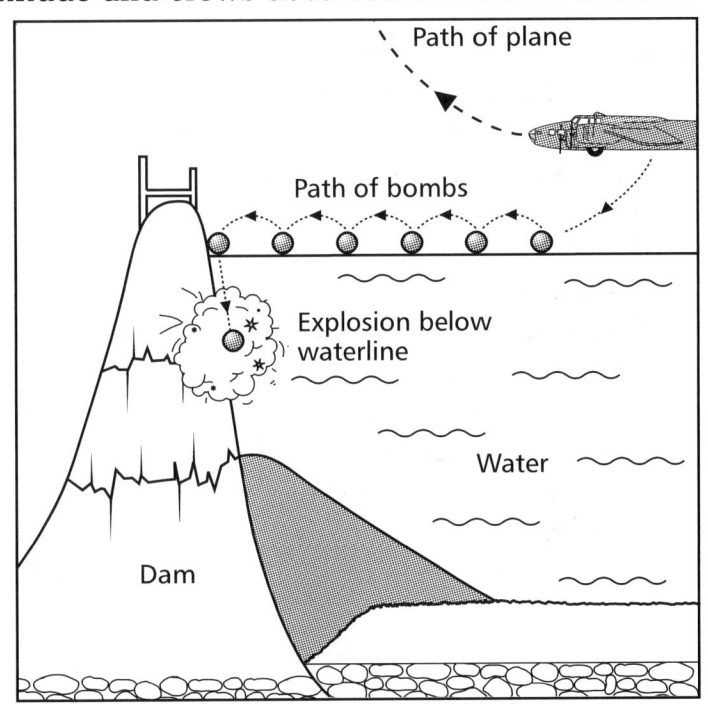

- Two dams were destroyed and industrial production was reduced for a while.
- Eight Lancasters were shot down and 53 aircrew were killed.
- Gibson won the Victoria Cross.
- The bouncing bomb was a brilliant invention and the raid was carried out with great skill and bravery.
- The RAF mistakenly believed that the Eder Dam's water fed into the Rühr. There was no value in destroying it.
- There were three other dams that fed the Rühr factories that the RAF never attacked.
- The raid was a great boost at the time to morale.
- The Sorpe Dam was built differently from the others and a bouncing bomb was the wrong weapon to use on it.

C / The Dambusters' raid (continued)

2 Each of the boxes on the previous sheets deals with one aspect of the Dambusters' story. Some boxes have headings to show which aspect is being covered. Write your own headings in the boxes that do not already have them.

3 Work in pairs. One of you supports the view that the raid was worth it, and the other that it was not worth it. Write your report below.

The raid was worth it/The raid was not worth it

4 Discuss your report with your partner. Who has the strongest case? Explain your decision.

 A *Hitler's secret weapons*

Look at page 140 in your textbook.

1 Complete the boxes below.

V1 This was a pilotless _____ It was first launched in _____	**V2** This was a _____ It was first launched in _____

2 Complete the table below.

Name of weapon	Explosive used	Speed	Stoppable or unstoppable?
V1			
V2			

3 Look at the diagram of a V1 below to help to you to answer the questions on the next sheet.

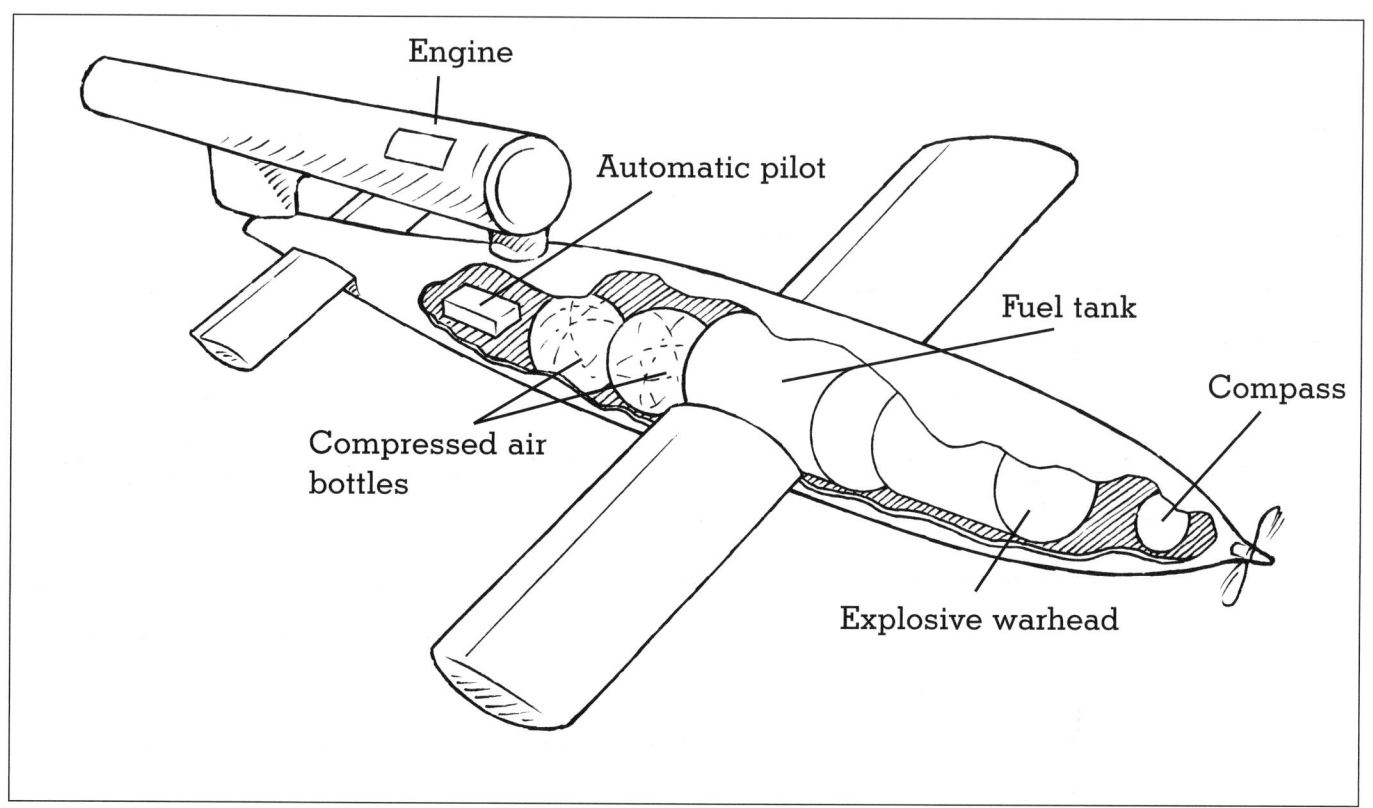

Engine
Automatic pilot
Fuel tank
Compass
Compressed air bottles
Explosive warhead

A Hitler's secret weapons (continued)

4 a Write down the names of the two parts of the V1 that helped it to fly.

_____

_____

b Write down the names of the two parts of the V1 that helped it to reach its target.

_____

_____

5 Look again at page 140 in your textbook.

a Which weapons (V1 or V2) killed most people?

_____

b Which city was the main target for V1s and V2s?

_____

c Approximately how many V2s hit Britain?

_____

d From which country were V1s launched?

_____

e From which country were V2s launched?

_____

f Write down anything that you think was done to try to stop V1s and V2s. Remember that most were launched after D-Day, when Allied soldiers had landed in France.

_____

_____

_____

B The bombing of Dresden

Look at page 137 in your textbook.

1 Study the sources below.

Source A ▶
A photograph of
Dresden after the
bombing raids in
February 1945

Source B Adapted from the writings of
Sir Arthur Harris in 1945. Harris was Head
of RAF bomber command.

▼

> Dresden was an important target... its
> destruction helped the Russian advance. The
> city had become the main centre of
> communications for Germany's defence... it
> had not been bombed in the war... it was a
> large producer of armaments.

Source C From a British newspaper
article written at the end of the war

▼

> German air raids on Britain throughout the
> war had not only been designed to reduce
> arms production, but also to terrorise the
> British public. The clearest example was the
> Luftwaffe raid on Coventry in 1940 that
> caused massive civilian casualties and
> widespread destruction of homes.

Source D From a survivor of Dresden

▼

> The day after the bombing ended I went
> off in search of my family. At first I saw
> only burnt parts of bodies being
> shovelled up into a big heap... later
> when I passed the women's clinic I saw
> female corpses, their torsos ripped open,
> their babies hanging half outside.

Source E Adapted from the views of a
historian writing in 1985

▼

> Every day that the war went on cost the lives of
> countless more Jews, Slavs and Poles. So the
> numbers killed at Dresden were nothing like so
> dreadful as the numbers of people Hitler was killing...
> a decisive blow was needed to end the war quickly.

B The bombing of Dresden (continued)

2 a Which sources contain views that **support** the Dresden raids?

_____

b Using the sources you chose for Question 2a, write a few sentences about why Dresden **should** have been bombed.

_____

_____

_____

3 a Which sources contain views that **oppose** the Dresden raids?

_____

b Using the sources you chose for Question 3a, write a few sentences about why Dresden **should not** have been bombed.

_____

_____

_____

4 Look again at your answers to Questions 2 and 3. Can you think of any reasons why the sources give different views? (Here are two possible reasons: they are by those actually involved in the event, or the writers have used different sources containing different information.)

_____

_____

_____

_____

_____

_____

_____

C *D-Day plans*

Pupil A: Sheet 1

**Only Pupil A should read this and the next sheet.
Do not use the textbook yet.**

Work in pairs. Pupil A has the job of devising a top secret plan for the Allied invasion of France in the summer of 1944.

1 Read the information below and on the next sheet about the resources at your disposal.

Sherman Duplex Drive tank – top secret!
With its rear propellers and top air bag, it can move for short distances in water.

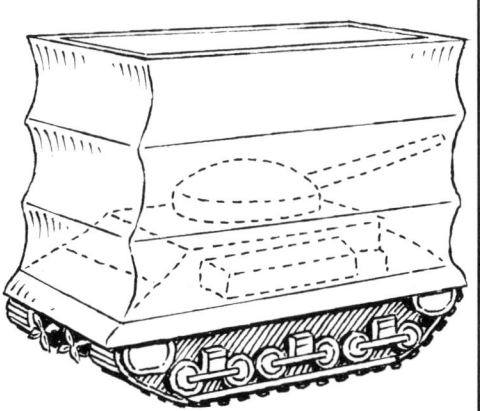

Mulberries – top secret!

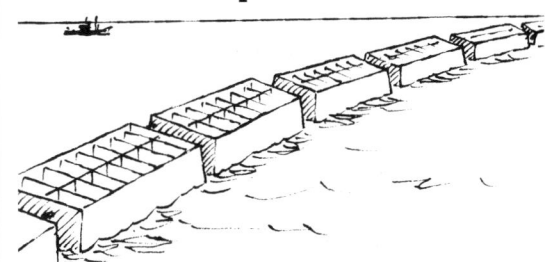

These are steel and concrete blocks containing hydraulically operated piers. They connect to land by pontoons (floating bridges). You can tow these across the Channel and they will become harbours.

Embarkation ports could be anywhere from Devon to Essex. The biggest ones are:
• Weymouth.
• Portsmouth.
• Southampton.
• Dover.

Pluto – top secret!
This is an underwater oil supply pipeline which can be laid across the Channel. You have 20 such pipelines.

'The Crab' – top secret!
This is a metal drum with chains attached, driven by a tank. The crab will flail the sand ahead to clear a path through minefields.

Churchill Bobbin tank – top secret!

This tank can lay a carpet of canvas to stop heavy vehicles getting bogged down in sand.

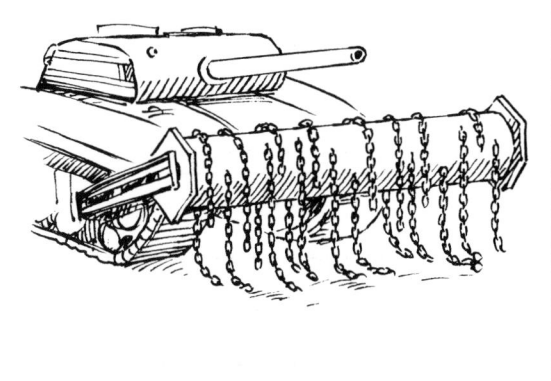

C D-Day plans (continued)

Pupil A: Sheet 2

German defences

They have 38 divisions of men spread out thinly and reasonably evenly along the entire French coast from Spain into Belgium. You do not know where their reserve tank divisions are. Information has been supplied by aerial reconnaissance and by the French Resistance.

Allied forces

- 39 divisions of armed forces.
- 11,000 combat aircraft.
- 2,300 transport planes.
- 5,300 warships and landing craft.

Deceiving the Germans

- Lieutenant Clifton James of the Army Pay Corps (and an amateur actor) is the double of Field Marshal Montgomery. The Germans know that no invasion of France can occur without Montgomery being in Britain at the time to supervise it. Could James be sent overseas, e.g. to North Africa, just before D-Day to give a false landing place?
- Dummy landing craft and tanks made of inflatable rubber are placed near Dover. If spotted by German reconnaissance planes, they would look real.

---

2 Plan your invasion. Remember to consider your resources and the need to fool the Germans over the location of the landings.

   a Should you land forces at ports or on beaches? Explain your answer, including details of the weapons/devices you want to use.

   _____

   _____

   _____

   b Do you want a shorter or a longer sea crossing? Explain your answer.

   _____

   _____

   _____

   _____

   c Where have you decided to land your forces?

   _____

   _____

C *D-Day plans (continued)*

Pupil B: Sheet 1

**Only Pupil B should read this and the next sheet.
Do not use the textbook yet.**

Work in pairs. Pupil B has the job of devising a top secret plan to defend France by German forces from an Allied invasion.

1   Read the information below about the resources at your disposal.

German forces
- 38 divisions of armed forces.
- These are deployed thinly along the French coast from the Spanish border into Belgium.

'Hedgehogs'
These are steel cones that can be embedded in sand to disable tanks and landing craft.

Mined rafts
These are large and can be half-submerged. They are capable of tearing the bottom out of landing craft.

Teller mines
These look like posts but contain enough explosive at the top to destroy a tank.

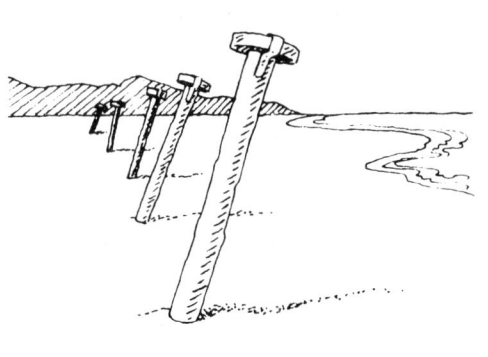

Intelligence reports
- Field Marshal Montgomery has recently (May 1944) been spotted in Gibraltar and North Africa. According to your secret agents, he was overheard suggesting southern France as the place for the Allied landings.
- Luftwaffe reconnaissance aircraft report sighting large numbers of landing craft and tanks being assembled near Dover.

Other forces
- You have a number of crack tank (Panzer) divisions in central France that can be moved to resist an Allied landing – but only if they are moved early enough.
- You have Luftwaffe squadrons that can easily bomb Allied ships in the Channel.

C D-Day plans (continued)

Pupil B: Sheet 2

2 Plan your resistance to the Allied invasion. Remember to consider your resources and the need to deploy them where you think the invasion will be.

  a Will the Allies land at ports or on beaches? Explain your answer, including details of the weapons/devices you want to use.

  _____

  _____

  _____

  _____

  _____

  _____

  _____

  _____

  _____

  _____

  _____

  b Will the Allies want a shorter or a longer sea crossing? Explain your answer, including details of weapons that might help your defences.

  _____

  _____

  _____

  c Where do you think the Allies will land? Where have you have decided to place the bulk of your defences?

  _____

  _____

  _____

  _____

D-Day plans (continued)

Pupil A: Sheet 3/Pupil B: Sheet 3

You should each have a copy of this sheet.

3   **Pupil A:** Mark on the map below: **a** the embarkation ports, **b** the route across the Channel, and **c** the landing sites.

   Pupil B: Mark on the map below: **a** your thin line of defences, and **b** where you would place your Panzas and Luftwaffe squadrons.

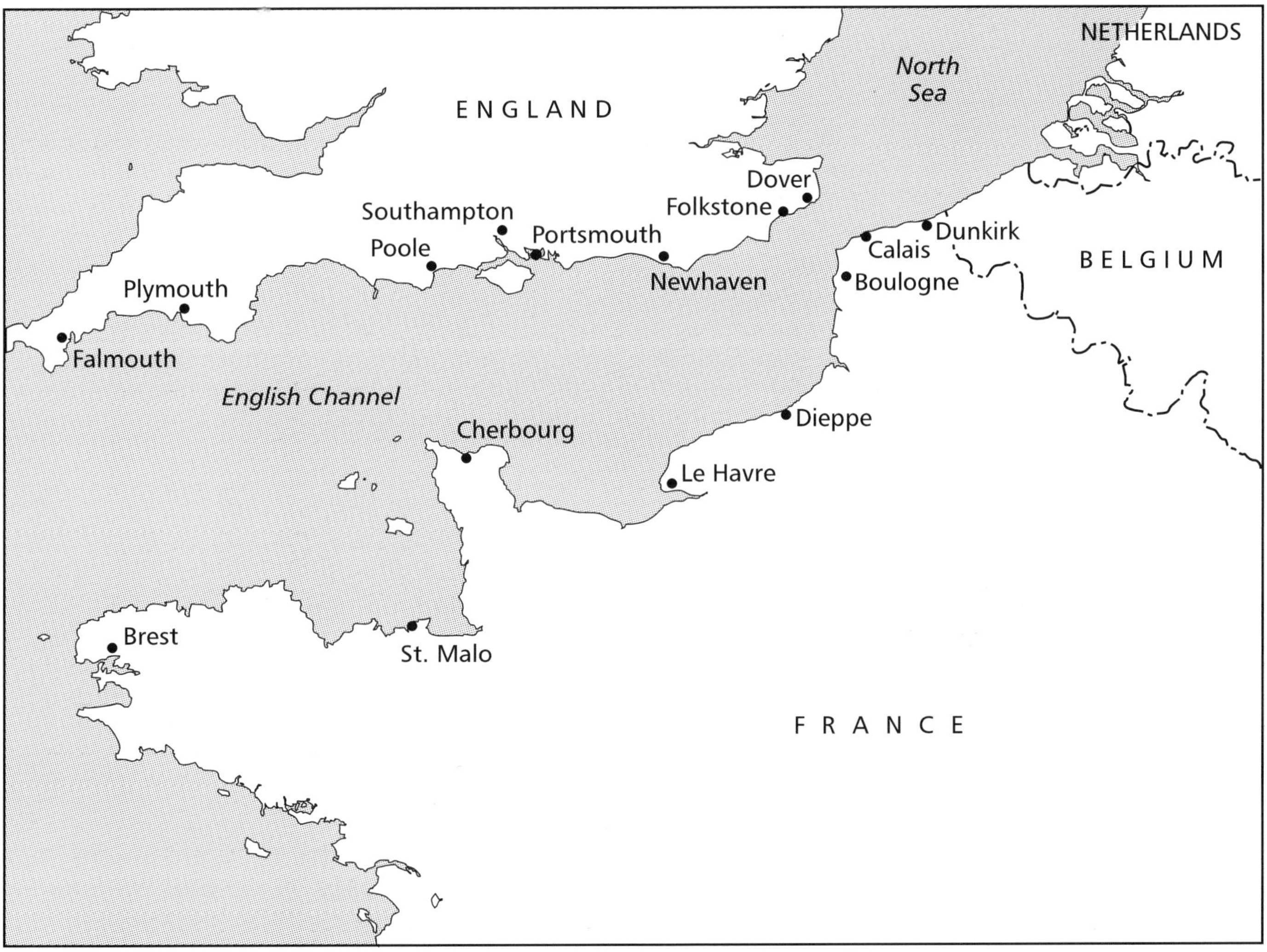

ENGLAND

NETHERLANDS

North Sea

Dover
Folkstone
Southampton
Portsmouth
Poole
Calais
Dunkirk
Newhaven
Boulogne
BELGIUM
Plymouth

Falmouth

English Channel

Dieppe
Cherbourg

Le Havre

Brest
St. Malo

FRANCE

4   Both of you should now read page 138 in your textbook to find out what really happened.

5   Look again at your plans. Who do you think would have won?

_____

_____

A Horror at Hiroshima

Look at page 146 in your textbook.

1 Study the picture below, which shows the B29 bomber nicknamed *Enola Gay*. This aeroplane dropped the atom bomb on Hiroshima on August 6, 1945.

In the first box at the bottom of the page are details of the jobs done by the flight crew. Using the job titles in the other box, work out which crew member's title goes with which job description and write these in the spaces provided on the aeroplane. One has been done for you.

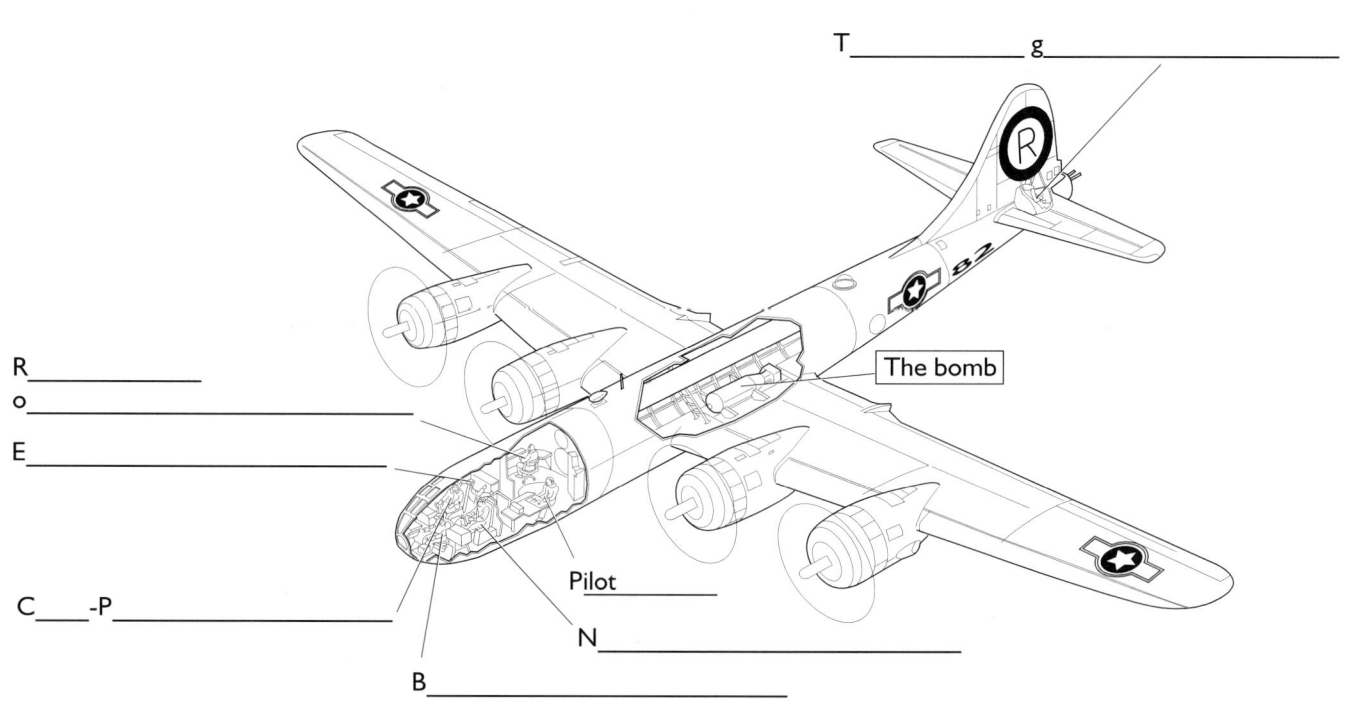

T_____ g_____

The bomb

R_____
o_____
E_____

Pilot_____

C___-P_____

N_____

B_____

Job descriptions
Aimed and released the bomb
Flew the aeroplane
Worked out the route to be flown
Fired on enemy aircraft
Sent and received messages
Checked the engines
Helped fly the aeroplane

Job titles
Co-pilot   Navigator
Bombardier   Tail gunner
~~Pilot~~
Engineer   Radio operator

 Horror at Hiroshima (continued)

2 Below is a diagram made up of three circles: the centre of Hiroshima, up to one mile away, and up to two miles away.

Write the words below about casualties in the correct circles.

35% killed instantly   0% killed instantly
100% killed instantly   0% died from radiation
25% died from radiation   50% died from radiation
Severe burns to skin   Mild burns to skin

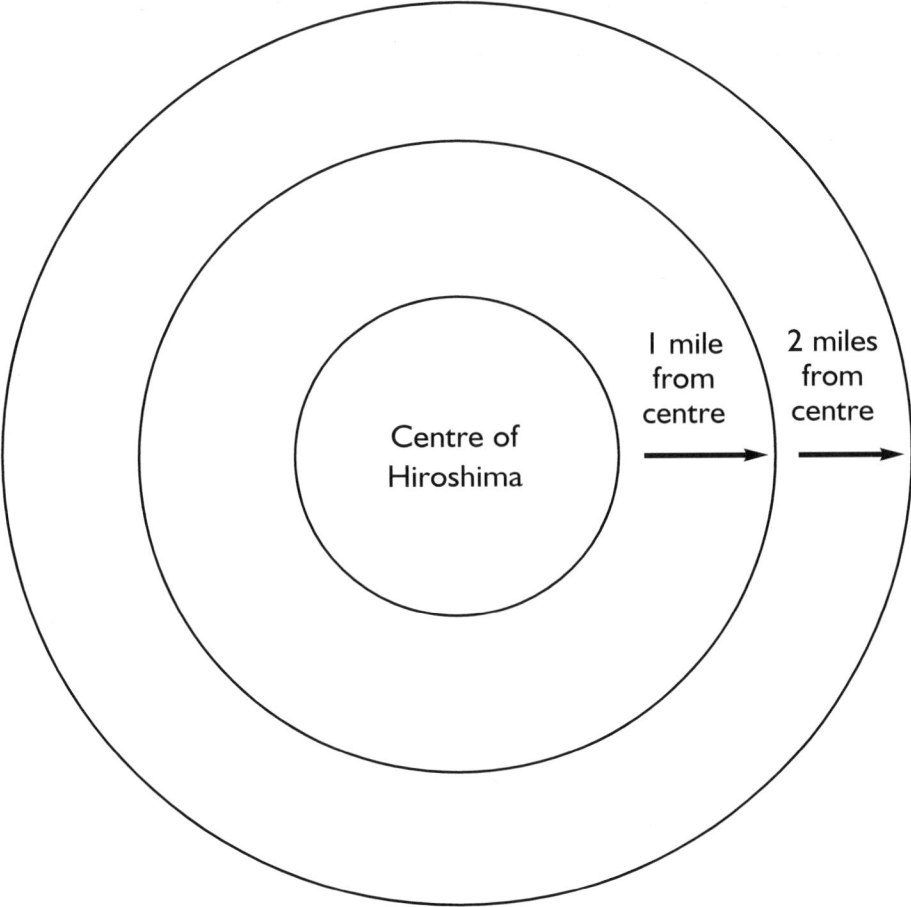

3 How many people lost their lives at Hiroshima?

_____

4 On which other Japanese city was an atom bomb dropped?

_____

5 What happened on September 2, 1945 because of the two atom bombs having been dropped?

_____

B The defeat of Japan

Look at pages 144 and 145 in your textbook.

1 Which country did most of the fighting against Japan?

_____

2 Write down the names of as many important naval battles in the Pacific between 1942 and 1945 as you can find.

_____

_____

3 Write down the names of two naval task forces involved in fighting the Japanese.

_____

4 What name was given to the strategy involved in recapturing Japanese-held islands?

_____

5 How could Japan be attacked after June 1945?

_____

6 What weapon was developed between 1942 and 1945?

_____

7 Which leader gave the order to use this new weapon?

_____

8 This new weapon was first used on August 6, 1945. On which city?

_____

9 The new weapon was used a second time on August 9, 1945. On which city?

_____

10 Which European nation had forces in South-East Asia in the war?

_____

B *The defeat of Japan (continued)*

11 Complete the diagram below. Try to find the best examples to write down.

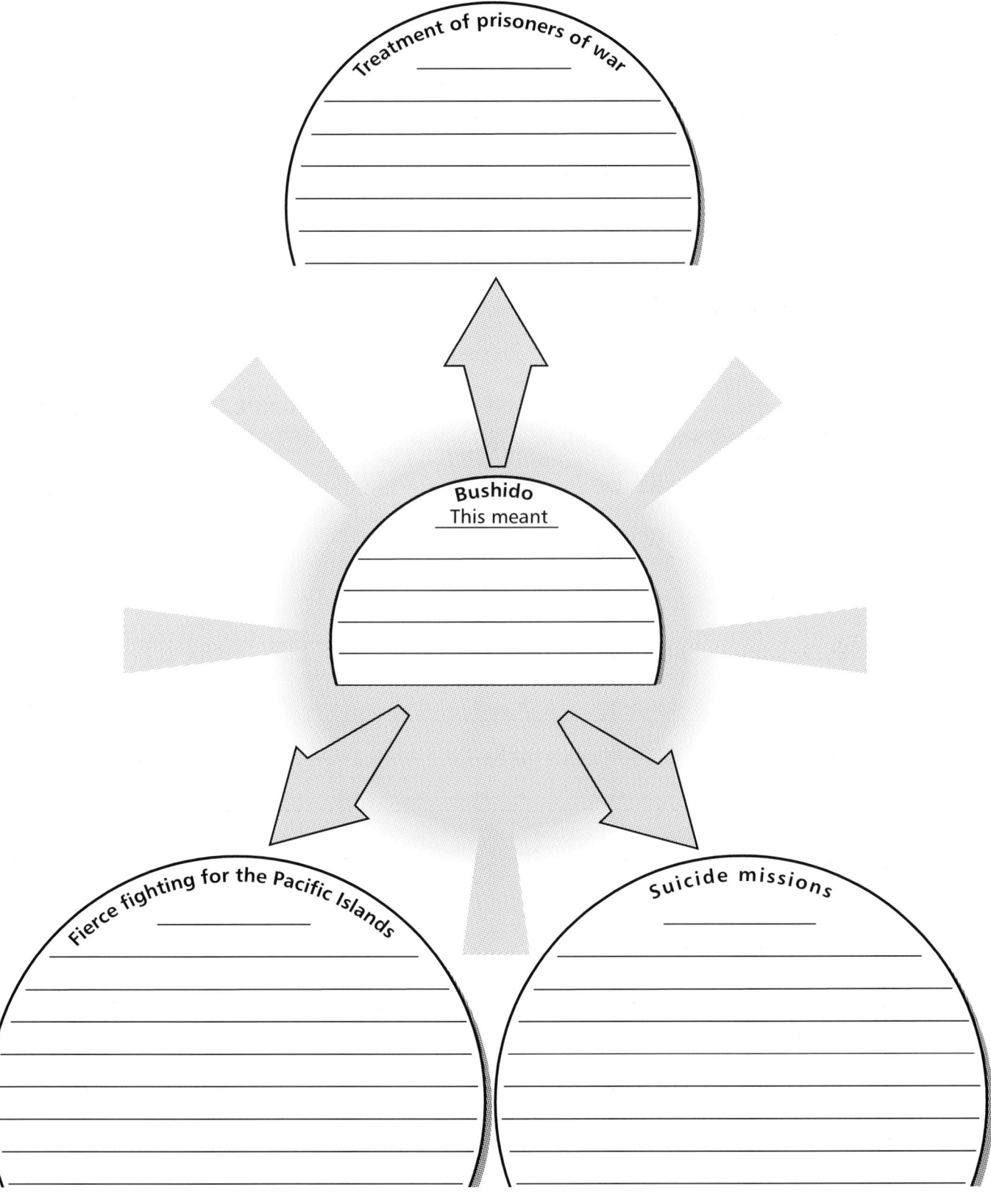

Treatment of prisoners of war
_____
_____
_____
_____
_____
_____

Bushido
This meant
_____
_____
_____
_____

Fierce fighting for the Pacific Islands
_____
_____
_____
_____
_____
_____
_____

Suicide missions
_____
_____
_____
_____
_____
_____
_____

C The US victory in the Pacific

Look at pages 127 and 144 to 146 in your textbook.

You are going to write an essay to answer the question: 'How did the USA defeat Japan in the Pacific in the Second World War?'

Read the paragraph box headings below (they are in no particular order).

US island hopping and bombing raids • Effects of atom bomb • Turning points in 1942 • Use of atom bomb • Japanese military resistance • The situation in the Pacific by 1941

1   Decide which of the above headings is the Introduction and which is the Conclusion.

2   Work out an appropriate order for the other headings (e.g. chronological).

3   Write the headings in the spaces at the top of each box.

4   Write your essay by:

    a   putting important relevant information into appropriate boxes.

    b   defining each of these key terms and putting them in appropriate boxes: island hopping, bushido, kamikaze.

Introduction

_____

_____

_____

_____

_____

_____

_____

_____

_____

_____

You will need

C The US victory in the Pacific (continued)

Conclusion

A *Stanley Hollis*

Look at page 138 in your textbook.

1   Read the factfile below.

Factfile

Company Sergeant Major Stanley Hollis

- Stanley Hollis was a company Sergeant Major in the Green Howards Regiment.
- He had already been praised for capturing a German machine-gun post on his own in Sicily in 1943.
- On D-Day (June 6, 1944) Hollis and his men landed on King's Beach in Normandy.
- They came under very heavy fire, and many men were killed as soon as they left their landing craft.
- On his own and firing a sten gun, Hollis rushed straight at a German machine-gun pillbox. He leapt on the roof and threw a hand grenade inside, killing most of the soldiers.
- He then forced all Germans in a trench to surrender.
- These actions allowed his company to get off the beach and move inland.
- Later on the same day he discovered a German field gun in an orchard packed with enemy troops. Despite coming under heavy fire, he destroyed the weapon with an anti-tank gun. Then he rescued two of his men.
- For his actions he was awarded the VC (Victoria Cross) medal.

You will need

 Stanley Hollis (continued)

2   Using the factfile on the previous sheet, colour around any areas of information that show only Hollis's actions.

3   Complete the table below, which is like a school report. Remember that in the Grade column, **A** is the best and **E** is the worst.

Report on Stanley Hollis			
Place	Date	Actions	Grade (A–E)

You will need

ABC *What happened to your family?*

See if you can find out what happened to your ancestors in the Second World War. Here are some ways to find out:

- Ask members of your family – there may be photographs, letters, diaries, etc.
- Visit your local library or Public Record Office.
- Contact the following organisations, either by post or using a computer linked to the Internet:
  - the Army Records Centre, MOD, CS(RM)2B, Bourne Avenue, Hayes, Middlesex UB3 1RF.
  - the Commonwealth War Graves Commission (www.cwgc.org/).
  - the Imperial War Museum, Lambeth Road, London SE1 6HZ (www.iwm.org.uk/).
  - the Public Record Office, Ruskin Avenue, Kew, Surrey TW9 4DU (www.pro.gov.uk/).
  - the Royal British Legion (www.britishlegion.org.uk/).

Name	
Date of birth	
Names of close family members	
Education/childhood	
Job/career	

You will need

 *What happened to your family? (continued)*

Marriage/family

War service
      Regiment
      Rank
      Combat record

Injuries/death

 A *The start of the Cold War*

Look at page 148 in your textbook.

1 Complete the tables below.

Name of leader	Name of country
Franklin Roosevelt	
	USSR
Winston Churchill	
	USA
Clement Attlee	

The _____ Conference of February 1945	
Agreements	Disagreements

The _____ Conference of July 1945
Disagreements

2 Which of the major countries believed in communism?

_____

3 Which major countries were against communism?

_____

4 Name any three countries that got communist governments just after the end of the Second World War.

_____

You will need

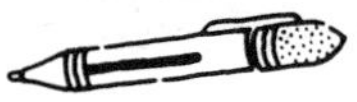

B The United Nations and the League of Nations

Look at pages 54 and 147 in your textbook.

1 Look at page 147 in your textbook.

a Which part of the UN organisation decides on policies?

____

b Which part of the UN organisation approves/disapproves policies?

____

c Which part of the UN organisation carries out policies?

____

d Complete the circles below by using examples from your textbook.

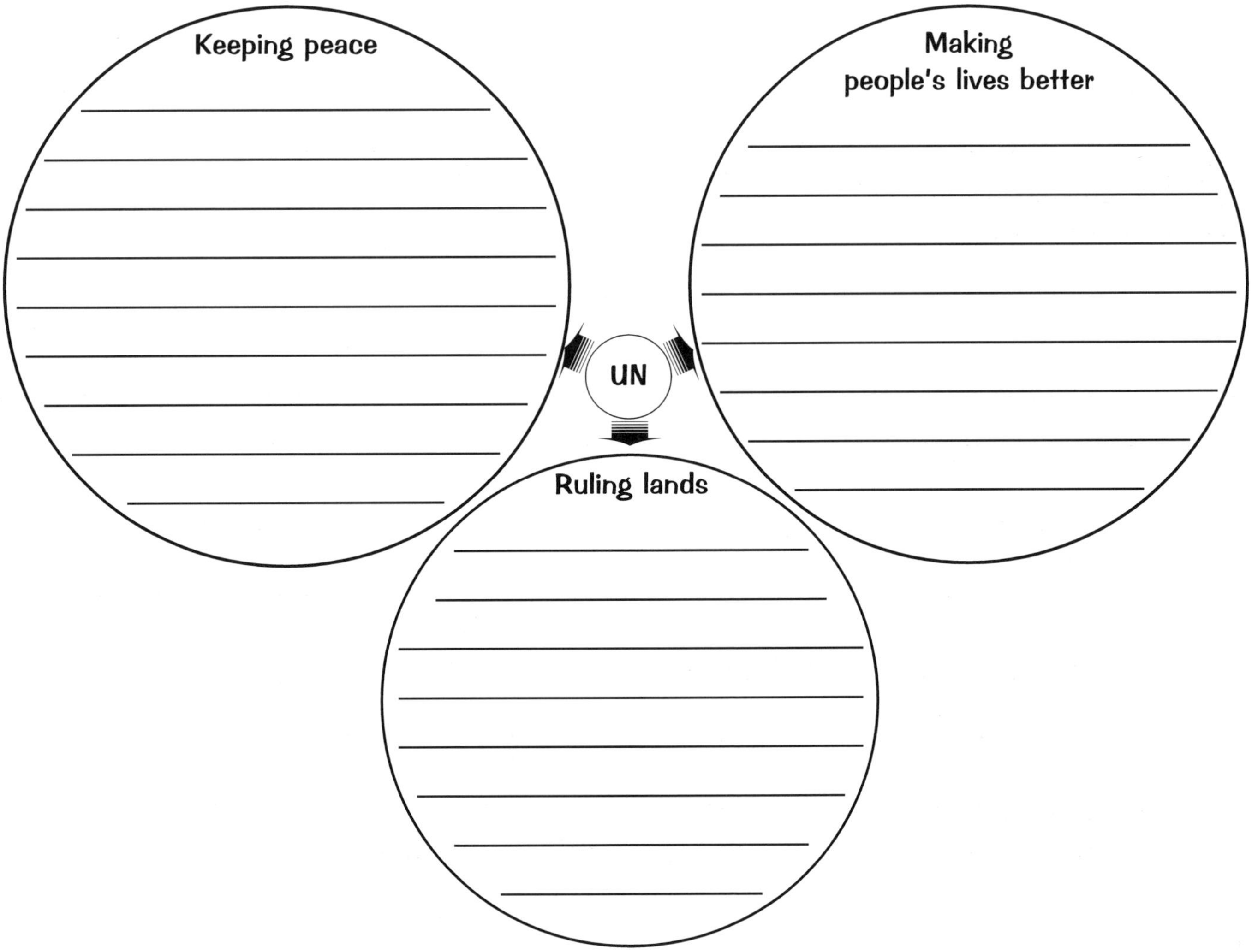
Keeping peace
Making people's lives better
UN
Ruling lands

B *The United Nations and the League of Nations (continued)*

2 Look at pages 54 and 147 in your textbook to compare the United Nations with the League of Nations.

a What similarities can you find about how both were organised?

_____

_____

_____

b What differences can you find about how both were organised?

_____

_____

_____

c What similarities can you find about how both tried to make people's lives better?

_____

_____

_____

_____

d What differences can you find about how both tried to make people's lives better?

_____

_____

_____

_____

_____

e What did the UN have concerning peace-keeping that the League of Nations did not have?

_____

_____

You will need
Dictionary

C *The two sides*

Look at pages 148 and 149 in your textbook.

1   Write a sentence to explain the term 'capitalism'.

_____

_____

2   Write a sentence to explain the term 'democracy'.

_____

_____

3   Write a sentence to explain the term 'communism'.

_____

_____

_____

4   What were the policies of the USA and USSR to each other immediately after the end of the Second World War?

_____

_____

_____

_____

_____

5   a Look again at the illustration on page 149. Use the information there to complete the tables below and on the next page.

Capitalism and democracy	
Benefits	**Drawbacks**

C The two sides (continued)

Communism	
Benefits	Drawbacks

b Look again at your tables. Why do you think the vertical lines dividing the two sections in each table has not been drawn in the middle?

_____

_____

_____

_____

_____

6 How did superpower relations deteriorate during the Cold War?

_____

_____

_____

_____

_____

_____

7 Why do you think the superpowers did not fight each other?

_____

_____

_____

_____

_____

_____

A The events of the Cold War

Look at pages 150 and 151 in your textbook.

1 Write down the year in which you think the Cold War began.

_____

2 Write down the year in which you think the Cold War ended.

_____

3 Write down the names of the two important countries who
   were enemies during the Cold War.

   a _____ b _____

4 Fill in the boxes below using examples from pages 150 and
   151 of your textbook.

When bad things happened	
e.g. more deadly weapons	**Wars/flashpoints**

When good things happened
e.g. less deadly weapons

5 What was there most of during the Cold War: good things or
   bad things?

_____

You will need

B Problems over Berlin

Look at pages 152 and 153 in your textbook.

1   It is June 1948 and the USSR has begun to cut off West Berlin
    from the Allies. Imagine you are a citizen of West Berlin
    worried about what the future may hold. Write a letter to an
    Allied commander outlining your fears and your suggestions
    for what action may be taken

Address _____

_____

_____

Date _____

Dear _____,

_____

_____

_____

_____

_____

_____

_____

_____

_____

_____

_____

_____

Yours _____,

_____

You will need

 Problems over Berlin (continued)

2 It is 1962 and the USSR has built a wall dividing West Berlin from the rest of the city. Imagine you are an East Berlin citizen who wants to live in West Berlin. Work out a plan about how you can escape from West Berlin. Remember to pay attention to the difficulties the wall will present.

My escape plan

The difficulties

_____

_____

_____

_____

_____

_____

_____

_____

_____

_____

My escape plan

_____

_____

_____

_____

_____

_____

_____

_____

_____

_____

_____

You will need

C Flashpoint Cuba

Look at pages 154 to 156 in your textbook.

1 Complete the table below using examples from pages 154 and 155 in your textbook.

Blame for the crisis	
Actions by the USSR	**Actions by the USA**
a	a
b	b
c	c
d	d

2 Look again at your table in Question 1.

    a Decide which action by each country was the **most** provocative and colour around these actions in the same colour.

    b Decide which action by each country was the **least** provocative and colour around these actions in another colour.

3 Do you think one side was more to blame than the other for the crisis? Explain your answer.

_____

_____

_____

_____

_____

_____

_____

_____

C Flashpoint Cuba (continued)

4 Look at the cartoon below, which suggests that Cuba was a trial of strength between Kennedy and Khruschev. Look at page 156 in your textbook to complete the thought bubbles for each leader. These should include what each was doing to worsen the crisis.

5 Consider the results of the crisis. If you had to redraw the cartoon, would either leader's hand be on the table? Explain your answer.

_____

_____

_____

_____

A Now you have finished

Look again at your textbook to help you answer the following questions.

1 a What was your favourite illustration from the textbook.

_____

b Write down a reason why you like this illustration.

_____

2 a Name a person whom you particularly liked or admired.

_____

b Write down a reason why you liked this person.

_____

3 a Name a person whom you particularly disliked.

_____

b Write down a reason why you disliked this person.

_____

4 a Work out which chapters contained topics where good things happened to people.

  b Write these titles next to the tick in the box below.

5 a Work out which chapters contained topics where bad things happened to people.

  b Write these titles next to the cross in the box below.

✓	✗

B A *last look at the textbook*

Look again at your textbook and/or your answers to the questions in the worksheet on page 9: 'A look at the textbook'.

1 a Which topics do you think turned out to be the most important?

_____

b Write a sentence to explain why these topics were important.

_____

2 a Which topics do you think turned out to be the least important?

_____

b Write a sentence to explain why these topics were not important.

_____

3 Were the most important topics given the most chapters, and the least important topics the fewest chapters?

_____

4 Did the people you chose end up being the most important?

_____

5 a Which other people were important in the 20th century?

_____

b Write a sentence to explain why one of these people was important.

_____

6 Do you think the front cover introduces 20th-century topics well?

_____

_____

C *What did we study?*

Look again at your textbook and/or your answers to the questions in the worksheet on pages 10 and 11: 'What are we going to study?'

1   Do you think the topics with the most pages allocated to them turned out to be the most important in the history of the 20th century? Give reasons for your answer.

_____

_____

_____

2   Do you think the author's choice of illustration for the front cover of the book turned out to be appropriate? Mention any other aspect of the 20th century that might have been included.

_____

_____

3   Was your choice of the six most important people accurate? Are there any others you might have included?

_____

_____

4   How much have the different items (e.g. illustrations) on each double page helped you to learn about 20th-century history? Explain your answer.

_____

_____

5   Which events of the 20th century do you think represent progress for mankind?

_____

_____

6   Which events of the 20th century do you think represent regression for mankind?

_____

_____